THE MANAGEMENT OF

MARINE FISHERIES

THE MANAGEMENT OF
MARINE FISHERIES

BY

J. A. GULLAND

Department of Fisheries, F.A.O., Rome

UNIVERSITY OF WASHINGTON PRESS
SEATTLE

1974

© SCIENTECHNICA (PUBLISHERS) LTD., 1974

Distributed in the United States of America by
University of Washington Press, Seattle

Library of Congress Cataloging in Publication Data

Gulland, J   A
     The management of marine fisheries.

     Bibliography: p.
     1.   Fishery management.   I.   Title.
SH328.G84   1974   338.3'72'7   74-2473
ISBN 0-295-95335-7

PRINTED IN GREAT BRITAIN BY HENRY LING LTD., A SUBSIDIARY OF JOHN WRIGHT
AND SONS LTD., AT THE DORSET PRESS, DORCHESTER

PREFACE

The management of marine fisheries presents a complex mixture of biological, economic, social, and political problems. In recent years this subject has earned increasing attention owing both to the growing pressures on the world fish stocks, and to the general concern with the proper use of the environment, of which the rational harvesting of fish in the sea is an important special case.

The catch of fish (including whales) from the sea has been doubling every decade, and now amounts to some 65 million tons of high quality protein. These fish provide a major source of animal protein in many countries, and for a few, such as Iceland or Peru, fish and fish products are major foreign currency earnings. A substantial increase in harvest is still possible, but an increasing number of stocks are becoming heavily exploited, and their continuing productivity will only be assured, and the well-being of the fishermen and the fishing industries be maintained, if the fisheries are properly managed.

The concern of the general public with the proper use of the natural resources of the sea has been most marked in the case of whales. Though this concern for whales, most clearly expressed at the United Nations Conference on the Human Environment at Stockholm in 1972, has arisen, as described in Chapter 2, some years after the main crisis in Antarctic whaling had been largely resolved, the general concern for the responsible use of the ocean's living resources is bound to grow.

Such use can only be achieved by the combination of expertise from several fields—the natural sciences to determine what is happening to the fish stocks in the sea and the effects on the fish stocks of different actions, economics and social sciences to determine the long and short-term effects of these actions on the fishermen and on society generally, and, often, political and diplomatic skills to put the necessary actions into effect.

In writing this book I have drawn deeply on my experience in these matters at the Fisheries Laboratory at Lowestoft, and with the Food and Agriculture Organization of the United Nations in

Rome. I owe a large debt of gratitude to my colleagues at Lowestoft and Rome and elsewhere around the world, particularly from talks and discussions at numerous meetings of international commissions, councils, and working parties as far apart as Lima, Abidjan, and Wellington. From them I have gained many of the ideas and concepts described here, though any errors of interpretation are mine. Also the views are mine, and not necessarily those of F.A.O. In this book I have attempted to cover, at least in outline, all the main aspects. Inevitably, given my interests and experience, more space has been given to the biological questions of understanding events in the fish stocks in the sea—though I also believe that these present some of the most difficult and the most interesting problems relating to fishery management. However, it is hoped that the book will be of interest to many others besides fishery biologists and will enable administrator, economist, or industrialist concerned with specific elements of the fishery world to understand the contribution of other specialist fields to the ultimate objective of thriving and well-managed fisheries throughout the world.

Rome   J. A. G.
June, 1973

CONTENTS

This book is the first of a series of monographs in Marine Science.

General Editor: F. R. Harden Jones

Chapter

1

THE PROBLEM OF FISHERY MANAGEMENT

THE management of marine fisheries, to ensure the best use of what are now recognized as the limited, if very large, resources of the ocean, has become one of the major problems facing fishery scientists and others. The term 'management' gives an impression of a strong positive controlling agency, with a managing director in charge of the North Sea plaice fisheries, with day-to-day responsibility for determining how much plaice are caught, where, and of what sizes. Fishery management may be struggling slowly in this direction, but in the past it has been mainly a matter of restrictive regulations introduced to minimize the harmful effects of too much of the wrong kind of fishing.

What constitutes harm, or the wrong kind of fishing, has often been a matter of opinion, with greatest weight given to the opinion of established fishermen. Since most fishermen are convinced that all other groups of fishermen, whether from the next village or from the next country, are foreigners intent on ruining their livelihood, management has often been the excuse for marine Luddism, in which the new and efficient gear is banned in the name of conservation. Jealousy and fear of new methods were the reasons for the prohibition of the use of the trawl or 'wondyrechoun' in the Thames Estuary in the reign of Edward III, some 700 years ago, just as they are for the prohibition of such effective gear as monofilament gillnets in many fisheries today. In the latter case there is in fact the additional justification that uncontrolled use of the more effective gear would result in damage to the stocks, and it may be easier (if less efficient) to prohibit the use of the better gear completely, rather than control the extent of its use.

The early restrictive measures of management generally applied to small coastal areas where the conflict between gears was most severe. On the high seas, fishermen and fishing nations behaved as though the resource was unlimited, and management measures were unnecessary. Until the power of the engine was added to sail and man-power to increasing the effectiveness of fishing gear, this assumption was broadly true. However, soon after steam trawling was introduced into the North Sea toward the end of the last century, falling catches per unit effort (catch per day or per trip) and a halt to the rise in total catch showed that the resources of the most valuable and vulnerable bottom fish, such as plaice, were indeed limited.

These fish stocks were mostly outside the limits of national jurisdiction, and were often exploited by several countries. The implementation of any management measure required more than the response of a single national administration to the demands of special groups. Rather, it was necessary to persuade several, often diverse, groups to agree on the need for action. The effective basis of such persuasion has been adequate scientific investigation. The decline of fish stocks has therefore been the trigger for much national and international research. Following the decline in catch rates in the North Sea, the International Council for the Exploration of the Sea (I.C.E.S.) was set up in 1906. With its headquarters in Copenhagen, it has been a model for international coordination of research, with nearly all the actual work being carried out at the national level. I.C.E.S. has always been a scientific body though with much, but by no means all, of its work directed to questions of overfishing and management. International action toward the actual implementation of specific management measures did not start until nearly half a century later, and has been effected by other intergovernmental bodies. Research and management have been more closely linked in the Pacific. After the first world war the stocks of the Pacific halibut became seriously depleted. An international body from Canada and the U.S.A. was set up. This body, now the International Pacific Halibut Commission, is responsible both for carrying out the relevant research and for proposing any regulations that appear to be necessary.

This second age of fishery management, in which management regulations based on clear and definite scientific evidence replaced the interest of established pressure groups, reached its peak in the 1960s. In this period the emphasis on biological knowledge had often resulted in the objective of management being defined solely in biological terms—the attainment of the maximum sustained physical yield—and in management action being refused in the absence of conclusive scientific evidence. It is now being recognized that such definitions of an objective, and the corresponding conditions for management, are too narrow and restrictive. A fishery may get into grave social or economic difficulties even when the physical yield is maintained; conclusive scientific evidence may be difficult to establish, or take so long to establish in a fast-developing fishery that the stock of fish and the fishery on it are badly damaged before the evidence is conclusive and the appropriate remedial action can be taken. This attitude of considering management action to be entirely determined by the results of biological analysis is now being replaced by one in which fishery management, in the sense used here, is considered much more as a specialized, but not entirely abnormal, case of management in general.

A trend toward considering management (in the sense of regulations) as just one aspect of managing fisheries (in the business management sense) has been aided by the increasing involvement of governments in the fishing business. The most obvious example is the great fleets of long-range factory ships operated by the U.S.S.R., Poland, and other centrally planned countries. In many other countries—Korea, Ceylon, etc.—the development of modern fishing industries has to a considerable extent been carried out by government financed and controlled fishing corporations.

Clearly, the business decisions taken by governments on future investment policy, the allocation of fishing fleets to different grounds, etc., should take into account *inter alia* the effects that these actions will have on the stocks and hence on future catches, which are the same considerations as are involved in the framing of regulations. Consideration of the needs of management (in the narrow sense) are therefore one, if often a very important, element in the decision-taking process.

Paradoxically, some reduced emphasis on purely biological evidence in deciding on management action has been made possible by the past persuasiveness of the scientific case. It is now fully accepted that all fish stocks are limited, so that a mass of data concerning declining catch rates of, say, hake off South Africa, are not necessary before those fishing that stock can be persuaded that regulation in the hake fishery might be necessary. Arguments indeed may arise about whether the point at which management must be introduced has been reached or not.

3

These arguments essentially concern the comparative losses brought about by introducing management measures too early (before the stock is fully exploited) and too late (after it has been seriously depleted, or economic damage has been done to the industry). These will depend on the type of management measures being considered and their likely effects on the fishing industry, as well as the biological evidence, and the possible uncertainties in it.

A new concept of fishery management is taking shape, arising from these shortcomings of management based purely on an objective in biological terms (maximum physical yield). It is not yet possible to offer a concise definition to replace the maximum sustainable yield as the objective—'maximum net economic yield'. introduces almost as many difficulties as it solves; instead, some rather more diffuse objective as 'the best possible use of the resource in the interests of the community as a whole' may have to be adopted.

All decisions concerning the fishery would be taken with this objective in view. At first, action would be primarily toward encouraging the development of the fishery. Later, as the limit of the fish stock was approached, development would be slowed down, and the decisions would become mainly concerned with restrictive management (in the narrow sense). However, the measures should at all stages maintain the operating efficiency of the fishery and the restrictions would be more concerned with discouraging or preventing the entry of excess resources of men, capital, vessels, etc., into the fishery than with the activities of those already engaged.

Whatever the pattern and objectives of management, the question of ownership and jurisdiction has been critical. If fish resources were under single ownership, management would raise few major problems. There would be some scientific work in advising on the best management policy, but the great problems of reaching decisions on what limits should be set to the amount of fishing, and how these limits should be achieved, would be dealt with as part of the complete procedure of managing fish business, of which the fish resources would be a major capital asset. Excess amounts of fishing would not be used because the owner would realize (given reasonable scientific advice) that the real addition to the total production by this extra effort, the marginal yield, would be small or even negative (Gulland, 1969).

4

With a few minor exceptions, e.g. some oyster grounds, fish stocks are not owned. Usually a number of different enterprises exploit the same resource.

The decision to add another vessel to the fishing fleet is based on an assessment of whether that vessel will catch enough to make its own individual operation profitable, rather than whether it adds enough to the total catch. Since the extra vessel will reduce the stocks and hence, to some extent, the catches by all other vessels, the marginal yield will always be less than the catch of the extra vessel. Extra vessels will therefore be added to the fleet after the time where no more expansion would have occurred under single ownership. This is true whether the competing enterprises come from different countries in a high seas, multi-national fishery, or from different companies in a fishery on a stock occurring in waters under a single national jurisdiction.

While placing a fish stock under a single national jurisdiction does not offer a complete answer to the problems of management —and it has been suggested (McKernan, 1972) that under certain circumstances international management has been more successful than national—disputes over national jurisdiction have been a striking feature of international fisheries. A partial list includes the Anglo–Icelandic 'cod war', the dispute between the U.S.A. and Latin-American states (principally Peru and Ecuador) over tuna, between France and Brazil over lobster, between Japan and Canada and the U.S.A. over salmon in the Pacific, and between Denmark and several other countries over salmon fishing at Greenland.

While many of these disputes had their origin in the earliest and most selfish form of management—clearly expressed by Cushing as 'sink every other man's boat but mine'—they mostly became explained and justified in terms of the second stage of management, based on scientific principles. Good advice on the biological and other aspects of fishery management has helped to resolve these conflicts, which have sometimes, e.g. between the U.S.A. and Ecuador–Peru, invoked international disputes and ill feeling far in excess of the issues at stake.

The varying approaches to fishery management, and the varying success with which the obstacles to complete and effective management have been overcome, are reflected in the history of different fisheries. These range from almost completely successful management to almost equally complete failure.

The best example of successful management of an international fishery resource is the North Pacific fur seal—assuming, as is usually done, that the term 'fishery' should include the exploitation of whales and seals. By 1911 unrestricted hunting of fur seals on the high seas and on the limited number of islands in the Bering Sea on which they bred, had reduced the stock to a small fraction (about 120,000 animals) of their original numbers. Kipling's story of the White Seal tells the story vividly from the seal's point of view although there was no secret island to give them sanctuary. Instead, an agreement between the four countries concerned (Japan, U.S.S.R., U.S.A., and U.K. on behalf of Canada), prohibited killing of seals on the high seas, and put the harvesting of animals on the breeding islands under the strict control of the Governments concerned (U.S.A. and U.S.S.R.). In return for abstaining from pelagic (high-seas) sealing, Canada and Japan, who had no breeding islands, were given a share of the skins taken by U.S.A. and U.S.S.R. Under this arrangement, which has been renewed a number of times, and is now supervised by the International North Pacific Fur Seal Commission, the stocks have been rebuilt to a high level, and a substantial excess in value of furs over the costs of harvesting and administration is obtained.

A less successful management of marine mammals, that of whales in the Antarctic, is described in detail in a later section. Despite the existence of a management body, the International Whaling Commission, the stocks were allowed to decline to a very low level. Further decline has been halted, and the most depleted species (blue and humpback whales) are probably increasing slowly, but little is being done to rebuild the stocks of fin and sei whales on which the industry now depends (*see* Annual Reports of I.W.C.). The I.W.C. can, however, take some credit that the decline of the stocks has been halted early enough to support a continuing industry, even though it is a small one in comparison with the past or with what it could be under good management. This contrasts with examples of completely uncontrolled exploitation which resulted in the complete collapse of the industry, and the near or complete extinction of the animal concerned, e.g. right whales in the Arctic, the sea otter in the North Pacific, or the buffalo and passenger pigeon on land.

Fish stocks (in the narrower and precise biological sense) are generally less affected by excessive exploitation than mammals. They therefore offer fewer examples of complete collapse or of recovery under management. The classic example of a heavily fished stock has been the plaice and other bottom fish (cod, haddock, sole, etc.) in the North Sea. These stocks have been heavily fished for nearly a century—except for some respite during the two world wars—with no peace-time restriction on the amount of fishing. Catches have continued at a high level since complete international statistics began to be collected in 1906 (*see* the annual

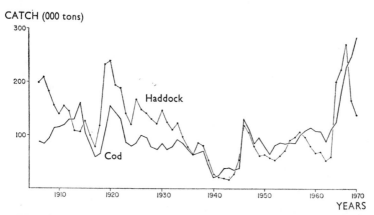

Fig. 1.—Total international catches of cod and haddock from the North Sea, 1906–69. Note drop in catches during the two wars, and absence of any long trend.

Bulletin Statistique of the International Council for the Exploitation of the Sea) (*Fig.* 1). Rather than any collapse, catches have recently tended to increase. The reasons for the increase are not well understood, though the general use of rather larger meshes in trawls and seines under international regulations that came into effect in the 1950s may have increased catches, especially of haddock and whiting, to some extent.

A mere absence of complete disaster does not mean that management is not desirable. Many studies (e.g., Graham, 1935; Beverton and Holt, 1957; Anon., 1957) have shown that a reduced level of fishing and a further increase in mesh size would give rather higher catches. Also, reduced fishing could allow the greater catches to be taken at a much reduced cost. To some extent, the level of fishing did fall after the second world war as investment in fisheries by the North Sea countries went into distant water fishing (England and Germany) or into industrial fish meal fishery (Denmark), and this had some beneficial effect on the stocks (Gulland, 1968). However, as these alternative resources have been depleted, the North Sea demersal fishing is tending to increase again.

Many other fisheries are tending toward the same state as the North Sea bottom fish—total catches not much less than the greatest possible, but taken at cost much above what is necessary. There have, however, been some spectacular collapses, such as that of the Californian sardine (*Fig. 2*). At one time among the biggest fisheries in the world, with a peak catch of 800,000 tons in

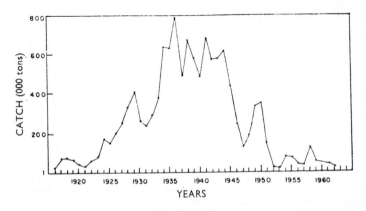

Fig. 2.—Catches of sardine along the Pacific coast of the United States. (*Data from* Murphy, 1966.)

the 1936/7 season, the stocks have now fallen to such a low level that no fishing for sardine was allowed in 1970. The reasons for the collapse have been in dispute (Marr, 1960), especially during the early stages of the collapse. It now seems fairly certain that the decline was aided, or indeed triggered off, by heavy fishing, though the continuation of the decline was ensured by the rise of the anchovy population (Murphy, 1966; Gulland, 1971). The uncertainty and disputes about the reason for the decline—a common theory was that it was entirely due to natural causes, possibly a change in water temperature—resulted in no effective management being carried out until the collapse was complete. The Californian sardine fishery is a monument to the failure to act in time, and to the insistence of having conclusive scientific evidence before acting.

REFERENCES

BEVERTON, R. J. H., and HOLT, S. J. (1957), 'On the dynamics of exploited fish populations', *Fish. Invest., Lond.*, ser. 2, **19**, 533.

GRAHAM, M. (1935), 'Modern theory of exploiting a fishery, and application to North Sea trawling', *J. Cons. int. Explor. Mer*, **13**(1), 76–90.

GULLAND, J. A. (1968), 'Recent changes in the North Sea plaice fishery', *J. Cons. int. Explor. Mer*, **31**(3), 305–22.

GULLAND, J. A. (1969), 'The concept of the marginal yield from exploited fish stocks', *J. Cons. int. Explor. Mer*, **32**(2), 256–61.

GULLAND, J. A. (1971), 'Ecological aspects of fishery research', *Adv. ecol. Res.*, **6**, 115–76.

MARR, J. C. (1960), 'The causes of major variations in the catch of the Pacific sardine *Sardinops caerulea* (Girard)', *in* Proceedings of the World Scientific Meeting on the Biology of Sardines and Related Species, *F.A.O. Fish. Rep.*, **3**, 667–91.

MCKERNAN, D. L. (1972), *National and International Fishery Management. 50th Anniversary of the College of Fisheries.* Seattle: Univ. Washington Press.

MURPHY, G. J. (1966), 'Population biology of Pacific sardine (*Sardinops caerulea*)', *Proc. Calif. Acad. Sci.*, **34**, 84.

ANON., (1957), 'International Fisheries Convention, 1946. Report of the *ad hoc* Committee established at the fourth meeting of the Permanent Commission, September, 1956', *J. Cons. int. Explor. Mer*, **23**(1), 7–37.

2

ANTARCTIC WHALING

ANY account of the management of marine fisheries must discuss the history of Antarctic whaling. This stands in the public mind, not entirely justly, as the foremost example of the failure to manage and conserve a resource. This public attention has been due to many things—particularly the drama of the pursuit of the largest animal that ever lived in the lonely Antarctic seas, and the political drama of the sessions of the International Whaling Commission around 1964, when the I.W.C. was faced by the need to take drastic action to conserve the resource.

THE WHALES

Four closely related species have been chiefly concerned—blue whales (*Balaenoptera musculus*), fin whales (*B. physalis*), sei whales (*B. borealis*), and humpback whales (*Megaptera nodosa*). All are baleen whales, which feed on small fish and planktonic animals by straining them out of the water with plates of baleen (whalebone) hanging from their upper jaws. Small numbers of sperm whales, the largest of the toothed whales, are also taken, especially at the beginning and the end of the season. These are not generally considered as an important element of the Antarctic industry, and catches of sperm whales are not included in calculating the catch limits set by the I.W.C. All four baleen whales are huge animals; the blue whale, the largest, may reach close to 100 ft. in length, and weigh over 100 tons, while even the relatively small sei whale can grow to nearly 60 ft., and weigh some 25 tons.

The pattern of movement and distribution is much the same for all species (Mackintosh, 1965). They move south in the beginning of the Antarctic summer (around November), and spend the summer feeding on the rich concentrations of small planktonic animals. Around April they move north again to spend the southern winter in the warmer temperate and subtropical waters, where they breed. Normally a mature female will produce one young every other year, though a female giving birth to a calf very early in one season may produce another one late in the following season, and twins occasionally occur—for instance of 1229 pregnant fin whales examined in the 1964/65 season, 10 contained twin foetuses. In the same season 4058 pregnant sei whales includes 61 pairs of twins and 5 sets of triplets. On the other hand, the mature female may miss a breeding season, giving birth only at three-year intervals.

The young whale grows fast. Gestation lasts rather less than a year, and at birth a young blue whale is about 20 ft. long, and a fin whale about 18 ft. (Laws, 1959). Growth after birth is about as fast, and the young whale reaches maturity (70–80 ft. long for a blue whale, and *c*. 60 ft. and 45 ft. for fin and sei whales respectively) at some 5 to 10 years of age. It appears that whales (or at least fin whales) are now maturing earlier (Lockyer, 1972), and also a higher proportion of the mature animals is pregnant (Laws, 1962) than in the early days of whaling. These changes are probably a reaction of the population to decreased density, and hence indirectly to exploitation. They are part of the mechanism whereby the stocks can maintain themselves under moderately heavy fishing, and thus whereby a certain level of yield (provided it is not too high) can be maintained indefinitely (Gulland, 1971).

In the absence of exploitation whales can live to a good age. Some doubts about the determination of the age of whales have only recently been removed (*see* Lockyer, 1972, and references therein), but it appears, from the examination of the number of layers in samples of ear-plugs, that fifty-year-old fin and sei whales are not infrequent. This is confirmed by the finding in the 1960s of several marks (small metal cylinders fired into the blubber of the whale, and recovered in the factory ship when the whale has been killed and is being processed), which had been applied to whales in the 1930s, some quarter of a century previously (Ohsumi, 1964).

The marking experiments have also shown that the migratory movements are rather strictly north and south, with little east–west dispersion. Thus the whales in the Antarctic fall into a number of rather separate stocks—southern Atlantic, south-western Indian Ocean, etc.—to refer to them in terms of their wintering areas. There is some latitudinal separation between the main areas of concentration of each species, though with some considerable overlap. Generally the blue whale is the most southerly, followed by the fin whale, with the sei whale farther north, in fact almost outside the Antarctic. The humpback is a special case. The other whales are oceanic animals, seldom coming close to shore. The humpback, especially in the winter, is a coastal animal. It forms a number of small, local, and at times highly concentrated stocks—the western Australian stock, the New Zealand stock, etc.—and these are highly vulnerable to excessive exploitation, both on their wintering grounds, and in the Antarctic, if the pelagic expedition should come across their concentrations.

This vulnerability of humpback whales has caused a cycle of events, which are almost perfect examples of the vicissitudes of unregulated fisheries, to be repeated in a number of places (West Africa, West Australia, etc.). First a shore station is set up to harvest the then abundant whales; for a few years good catches and good profits are made, but the stock is allowed to decline, and after a period catches fall to a level at which economic factors force the shore station to close. With luck enough whales are left, so that the stock can re-build; after a longer or shorter period the stock rebuilds to a level at which operations can start again, and the cycle repeats. Off Western Australia the cycle has been repeated four times, with large catches being taken at intervals of some fifteen years. In fact, if the stock is intrinsically so small that the sustainable annual catch is not enough to maintain a shore station in profitable operation, this pulse fishing may be the best way to harvest the resource. The important proviso is that operations cease while the stock is still large enough to recover quickly. This goes against much of the established practice of national fishery administrators who, faced with an industry in economic difficulties, tend to take such measures (e.g. low interest loans) as will encourage the industry to remain in operation. The result may then be that when at last even these measures have proved unable to keep the industry going the stock is so depleted that recovery may take a very long time, or may even fail to take place.

In the following discussion attention will be focused on the three main species—blue, fin, and sei—and the rather special case of humpback whales will not be treated in detail. In any case, the total population of humpbacks has always been small in relation to the others—excluding catches in temperate waters, the catches of Antarctic humpback whales in the last forty years have been under 30,000, compared with half a million fin whales and some 190,000 blue whales.

THE INDUSTRY

The history of Antarctic whaling, as shown by the statistics, set out in *Table* 1, started with a period of rapid expansion. This followed the development of the modern factory ship operation, in which the whales are hauled aboard up a stern slipway. The first of these, the *Lancing*, operated in 1925/26, and by the 1930/31 season forty-one pelagic factories with 200 catchers were in operation

Table 1.—BALEEN WHALE CATCHES IN THE ANTARCTIC (1924–25/1970–71)

Season*	Blue†	Fin	Sei	Season*	Blue†	Fin	Sei
1925	5,703	4,366	1	1950	6,182	20,060	1,284
1926	4,697	8,916	195	1951	7,048	19,456	886
1927	6,545	5,102	778	1952	5,130	22,527	530
1928	8,334	4,459	883	1953	3,870	22,867	621
1929	12,734	6,689	808	1954	2,697	27,659	1,029
				1955	2,176	28,624	569
1930	17,487	11,539	216	1956	1,614	27,958	560
1931	29,410	10,017	145	1957	1,512	27,757	1,692
1932	6,488	2,871	16	1958	1,690	27,473	3,309
1933	18,891	5,168	2	1959	1,192	27,128	2,421
1934	17,349	7,200	—				
1935	16,500	12,500	266	1960	1,239 (917)	27,575	4,309
1936	17,731	9,697	2	1961	1,744 (739)	28,761	5,102
1937	14,304	14,381	490	1962	1,118 (716)	27,099	5,196
1938	14,923	28,009	161	1963	947 (220)	18,668	5,503
1939	14,081	20,784	22	1964	112	14,422	8,695
				1965	20	7,811	20,380
1940	11,480	18,694	81	1966	1	2,536	17,587
1941	4,943	7,831	110	1967	4	2,893	12,368
1942	59	1,189	52	1968	—	2,155	10,357
1943	125	776	73	1969	—	3,020	5,776
1944	339	1,158	197				
1945	1,042	1,666	78	1970	—	3,002	5,857
1946	3,606	9,185	85	1971‡	—	2,888	6,151
1947	9,192	14,547	393				
1948	6,908	21,141	621				
1949	7,625	19,123	578				

* 1925 refers to the 1924/25 season, and so on.
† Including catches of pigmy blue whales; estimated catch of true blue whales shown in parentheses (1959/60–1962/63).
‡ Preliminary data.

(Mackintosh, 1965). Previous to this, Antarctic whaling had been confined to shore stations such as South Georgia, and to factory ships in which the whales were cut up in the water alongside the ship. This required sheltered water and was therefore possible only in certain areas.

At this time, and in fact until some time after the 1939-45 war, the predominant product from the whale was its oil—mainly obtained from the thick layer of blubber. Now a greater part of the value of a whale comes from other products—frozen meat (used for cat and dog foods and to an increasing extent for human consumption, especially in Japan), meat meal, etc. This has made some changes in the relative values of different species, in particular making the sei whale, which has relatively less blubber and more meat, become more attractive.

The basic method of operation has changed little in the past forty years. Each factory ship is attended by a number of catchers, often around half a dozen, though Russian fleets have used up to twenty catchers with each factory ship. In addition, the fleet includes a variety of auxiliary vessels such as tankers and refrigerated vessels for the frozen meat. Good records are kept of the number and position of all whales killed, as well as on the number and size of the catcher vessels and the number of days they have been in operation. These are reported to the Bureau of International Whaling Statistics in Norway, and the summarized data are published in the annual volumes of the *International Whaling Statistics*.

These data are invaluable in the scientific study of the whale stocks. One use of them is to deduce the relative abundance of whales: a useful first estimate of this is given by the catch per catcher-days-work, i.e. the total number of whales caught divided by the number of days on which catchers were hunting for whales (often estimated as the product of the length of the season in days, and the number of catchers, less a correction for days on which no catching was done, owing to bad weather, etc.). Over a period of years this is an unsatisfactory measure, because catchers have been more efficient—faster, bigger, with better equipment such as sonar—so that, for a fixed abundance of whales the catch per day would tend to increase. To correct for this, the increase in efficiency has been taken to be proportional to the observed increase in average gross tonnage of the catchers, and the abundance of whales estimated as the catch per catcher-ton-day

(Chapman, 1964), i.e. the catch-per-day divided by the mean tonnage of the catchers. This latter increased from a little over 300 gross tons in 1946 to some 750 tons now.

Once developed, Antarctic pelagic whaling expanded very rapidly and was principally directed at blue whales. Soon—by 1930—the industry was running into severe economic difficulties, and serious attention was given to some control of the total catch. Some of these difficulties were purely of economic origin—the greatly increased supply of whale oil on the depressed market of the 1930s brought prices very low.

However, the abundance of blue whales was already decreasing, and most of the industry (which at that time was dominated by Norwegians) were well aware of the history of whaling in other waters, in which uncontrolled hunting had resulted in the collapse of the stocks and the industries based on them. Those concerned in Antarctic whaling were therefore very conscious of the need for some form of management to ensure the continuing success of their operations. This, of course, as the subsequent history showed, did not ensure the immediate agreement to any specific measure. The critical factor has always been that any effective regulatory action needs to be taken more or less unanimously— otherwise all the benefit is obtained by those who do not restrict their activities. This unanimity in a multi-national industry in turn requires some international forum for discussion, in which agreements on the precise regulation can be reached.

THE FORMATION OF THE WHALING COMMISSION

During the pre-war period there were a number of attempts at international regulation of Antarctic whaling. These started with a League of Nations Convention for Regulation of Whaling, drawn up in 1931, which came into force in 1935. A more substantial step was the International Whaling Conference held in London in the summer of 1937, and attended by all the countries then engaged in Antarctic whaling, with the exception of Japan and Panama.

This Convention introduced a number of important regulatory measures, including the prohibition of the killing of grey and right whales, minimum size limits for blue whales (70 ft.), fin whales (55 ft.), humpback whales (35 ft.), and sperm whales; a prohibition on killing whales with calves; and a closed season for factory ships in the Antarctic from 7 April to 8 December. It also set rules to ensure the full utilization of all whales caught—they must be processed within thirty-six hours of being killed and the oil had to be extracted by boiling or otherwise from all parts of the whale (except internal organs, flippers, and whalebone). Previously, especially when the whales were dealt with alongside the factory ship, and not hauled on board, there were occasions where only blubber was used. The Convention also required that Governments should collect basic statistical information on the operations of the expeditions, including data on the species, sex, and length of all whales caught, and that this information should be reported to the International Bureau of Whaling Statistics in Norway. These data have been invaluable in the later scientific assessment of the whale stocks.

The Convention also gave definitions of various terms used, from which it may be noted that:

'fin whale' means any whale known by the name of common finback, common finner, common rorqual, finback, fin-whale, herring-whale, razorback, or true fin whale,

and

'grey-whale' means any whale known by the name of grey-whale, California grey, devil fish, hard head, mussel digger, grey back, or rip sack,

—a fairly comprehensive list. Perhaps not surprisingly, with this variety of English terms, the Convention did not attempt a corresponding list in any other language.

While the 1937 Conference was successful in the several important points outlined above, it was not successful in the most important: no restriction was placed on the total number of whales killed. This was appreciated by many of those concerned and a further conference was called in the summer of 1938, also in London. This noted that despite the hope expressed in paragraph 2 of the Final Act of the 1937 Conference, that it would 'go far towards maintaining the stock of whales, upon which the prosperity of the whaling industry depends', the actual number of whales caught in the 1937/38 Antarctic season (about 44,000) was some 10,000 in excess of the figures for the 1936/37 season.

In fact, the blue whale stocks were already in a very serious state, which was not shown by the figures of total catches, in which all species were added together. Despite a considerable increase in the amount of whaling—the numbers of catchers attached to the pelagic factory-ships increased from 184 in 1936/37 to 244 in

1937/38—the number of blue whales caught barely changed (14,183 in 1936/37, and 14,826 in 1937/38). The increase in total numbers caught was only achieved by greatly increased catches of fin-whales (nearly doubling from 13,302 in 1936/37 to 26,457 in 1937/38). The current situation of the blue whale stock, and the need for action were very clearly described in a resolution of the Whaling Committee of the International Council for the Exploration of the Sea (I.C.E.S.), at a meeting held in Copenhagen a month before the 1938 Conference, which stated that 'nothing less than a limitation of the total amount of whale oil that may be taken in any whaling season can be effective in preserving the stock of Blue Whales from being reduced to the level at which it can no longer be the object of economic exploitation'.

Later history has shown how right those scientists were.

The 1938 Conference was attended by representatives of thirteen countries, including this time Japan; the delegates included a future Prime Minister of Australia and a future Governor-General of Canada. It managed to tidy up some of the provisions of the 1937 Conference, but was unable to make substantial progress on the central question. A number of measures were considered:

a. Further shortening of the open season;
b. Limiting the number of catchers;
c. Limiting the total output during the season. If this was reached all whaling should cease;
d. Limiting the oil production per expedition;
e. Special measures for humpback whales;
f. The establishment of a sanctuary in waters south of 40° S.;
g. The closure of additional areas (outside the Antarctic) against pelagic whaling.

It was agreed that measures (*b*), (*c*) (which were the measures recommended by the I.C.E.S.), and (*d*) deserved further attention.

This attention was disrupted by the war, but negotiations continued with an informal meeting in July, 1939, and more formal conferences in January, 1944, and November, 1945. The war-time atmosphere must have removed short-sightedness and encouraged a more responsible attitude, because the 1944 Conference achieved the vital measure of setting an upper limit to Antarctic catches— 16,000 blue whale units (1 blue whale = 2 fin whales = 2½ humpback = 6 sei whales). This was very much below the catches in 1937/38 (about 25,000 B.W.U.). The more responsible attitude in this conference was shown by the preamble, in which it was noted that despite the critical shortage of oil and fats, which would be faced in the immediate post-war period, it was of vital importance that any relaxation of the existing agreements to meet this shortage should be for a limited period only, and shall ensure that existing stocks should not be decimated by unexpected developments.

The 1945 Conference confirmed the 16,000 limit, and proposed certain other measures. An interesting resolution, in view of the difficulties for any conservation agreement caused by the activities of nations not party to the agreement, was Resolution IV:

'That the various Governments should take all practicable steps to prohibit the sale, loan, or delivery of vessels, equipment, or supplies designed especially for whaling operations, or known to be intended for such operations, to any Government or nationals of any Government not a party or a signatory to the whaling agreement of 1937'.

No action ever seems to have been taken under the terms of this resolution. Like the formal protocols signed at the Conference, the resolutions were not ratified by the Governments concerned, since the arrangements for whaling regulations were taken over by the new International Whaling Commission, set up at the next year's conference. However, the resolution was an interesting, and perhaps important, first attempt to deal with the problem of new entrants to a fishery—in this case by trying to keep them out.

The disadvantage of the 1937 and later agreements until that of 1946 was that they contained no provision for a permanent body for overseeing the carrying out of the recommendations, or for the revision and, as necessary, amendment of the recommendations. To do this, the International Whaling Commission was set up, at the conference in Washington in December, 1946.

The Commission was given powers to recommend a wide range of management measures, including specifically the maximum catch to be taken in any one season, but excluding restrictions on the number or nationality of factory ships or land stations, and the allocation of specific quotas to ships or groups of ships. The latter exclusion has caused difficulties, and was overcome, as described later, by agreements among the Antarctic whaling countries outside the framework of the Commission.

The first decade after the war was the most successful that there has yet been in the management of whaling. Catches were limited to a level which in total was not much above the level that the stocks could withstand. There were, however, two major short-comings which in turn threatened the existence of the Commission, and nearly brought about the complete failure of effective management. The first was purely economic; while total catches were limited, the capacity of the fleets was not, and each season there was a rush to catch as much as possible, leading to a shorter and shorter season and progressively more costly operations. The second concerned the stocks; revision of the catch quota required the amendment of the schedule, and was in no way done automatically as the stocks fell. Thus, what in 1946 had been only a small difference between catch and sustainable yield (resulting in a very slow decrease in stock), had by 1955 become, through the decrease in the stocks, a big difference, and the stocks were falling rapidly.

It has also often been pointed out that the Commission should have set separate quotas for each species, rather than set a single quota expressed in blue whale units. Certainly the optimum scheme of management should include separate management régimes for each species—and indeed for each stock of each species, if the Antarctic whales of each species do not form as single homogenous stocks. A similar counsel of perfection has been urged for Pacific salmon, where the fish from each stream should be separately managed. Because fish from many streams mix in the rivers, and from several river systems mix in coastal waters, this perfection cannot easily be achieved. The real question is the degree to which any practicable management programme, falling short of the optimum, will produce less than optimum results. More specifically, in the case of the whales, the question is whether, given the two serious (and almost fatal) shortcomings—lack of allocation of quotas and difficulties in revision of the total quota—the additional failure to set separate quotas for each stock or each species made matters much worse.

A good case can be made out for the hypothesis that the use of the Blue Whale Unit system has actually improved the biological impact of the regulations since 1965. In this period the killing of both blue and humpback whales has been prohibited, so only two species have been reckoned in the B.W.U. quota. The fin whale stock had been depleted well below the level giving the maximum sustainable yield (M.S.Y.), while the sei whales were relatively lightly exploited, and abundance at least in 1965 was above the level giving the M.S.Y. The aim of management should therefore presumably have been to build up the fin whale stock, by taking less than the current sustainable yield, while allowing the sei whale stock to be thinned out to around the M.S.Y. level. (While the M.S.Y. level will only be exactly the optimum level under certain definitions of 'optimum', the economics of whaling are such that the optimum under nearly all realistic criteria will be very close to the M.S.Y. level.)

This differential treatment of the two species actually occurred in practice. The 3 : 1 ratio of the value of fin to sei whales implied by the B.W.U. system was set when oil was the predominant product. When meat and meat products became equally valuable, the relative value of sei whales increased, so that, with individual quotas set in B.W.U., it became desirable to catch sei whales rather than fin whales. Thus, in the 1967/68 season, when the sustainable yield of each species was about 5000 animals, the actual pelagic catches were 2152 fin whales, and 10,352 sei whales.

This happy effect was of course a matter of luck. It would have been achieved with more certainty if the Commission had explicitly decided to build up the fin whale stock, and reduce the sei whales, and had set species quotas accordingly. However, this would have been unlikely. The Commission might well have decided to set a sei whale quota that was higher than the sustainable yield, but would have been most unwilling to set a lower fin whale quota as an investment for the future—considerable pressure on the Commission at the time to set a lower B.W.U. quota for this purpose had been quite unsuccessful. An agreement to set separate species quotas would have therefore probably meant that more fin whales would have been killed, and made little difference to the sei whale catch.

There was in fact, during this period, a good example of mis-management through treating separate stocks together, rather than individually. This concerned the regional stocks of sei whales, which appear to be largely independent. Exploitation of these has been very uneven. The first stock to receive attention was that in the south-west Atlantic, from which some 22,000 whales were taken in the 1964/65 and 1965/66 seasons; by 1966 the stock had reached such a low level that less than 1000 whales were taken in the next three seasons. Thus in 1966 the Atlantic stock of sei whales was severely depleted, while those in the Indian and Pacific Oceans were hardly touched.

What would have happened earlier if species, rather than B.W.U. quotas, had been used, is more a matter of conjecture. If a change had been made between about 1955 and 1963, there would have been little effect, since the catches were almost entirely fin whales, but a change around 1950 might have had results. At that time the stock of fin whales was not far from the optimum level, and the catch close to the maximum sustained yield. If the catch could have been kept at this level (at rather below 20,000 whales per year) all would have been well. However, the blue whales were being steadily fished down, and as they became fewer and harder to catch, increasing fin whales were taken to maintain the B.W.U. quota. Thus species quotas would have benefitted the fin whales greatly, though possibly at the cost of an even faster collapse of the blue whale stock, though this would have depended on whether the Commission would have been more willing to reduce a blue whale quota, in the face of falling abundance, than it was in practice to reduce a B.W.U. quota.

This is entirely hypothetical. In fact the Commission, though aware of the theoretical and biological advantages of species quotas, was unwilling to adopt them. The interesting point arising from these speculations is that no single measure, even such a theoretically desirable one as separate quotas for each stock, can be considered in isolation. In the 1950s they could probably have helped; in the late 1960s they could have hindered.

THE DIVISION OF THE QUOTA

Of the two weaknesses that lay at the heart of the Commission —no allocation of the quota, and no semi-automatic revision of the overall quota to take into account changes in abundance—the former was the first to be seriously tackled. As discussed later, the solution of the second problem largely depended on a prior solution to the first. Soon after the Commission came into operation, and there was an effective brake on whaling operations, the economic losses involved in managing by a single overall quota became apparent. In the 1946/47 season—the first reasonably normal post-war season—15 factory ships operated with 129 catcher vessels—an average of 8·6 per expedition—and operations lasted 121 days, with a catch of 15,300 B.W.U. Five years later the number of expeditions had increased slightly to 19, but the catchers had doubled, and the length of season had shrunk to 64 days. The whole complex equipment of a pelagic expedition could therefore be used for barely two months each year, but during that time it had to be used flat out around the clock—weather and whales permitting.

While these were hardly conditions to allow any business to operate efficiently, no expedition manager could afford to relax the pace of operations or his share of the total catch would fall. On the contrary, his only hope of a profitable season was to operate more intensively, by attaching more and more powerful catchers to the expedition, in the hope of catching and processing enough whales in the short season to cover the heavy fixed costs. The situation was similar to that in any unmanaged resource, for which any unilateral move to reduce the catch results in benefits for everyone, except the man making the reduction. Any move to reduce the excess capacity of the increasing number of ever larger catchers which was not nearly unanimous, would only benefit those who did not make the reduction.

At the Tenth meeting of the Commission in 1958 the U.K. Commissioner therefore proposed (*see* Tenth Annual Report of the Commission) that the nations concerned should consult among themselves how to solve this economic problem, possibly by an agreement on sharing the catch. He pointed out that until the economic problems were solved it was difficult to agree on any reduction in the overall quota, though this was becoming more clearly seen to be desirable. If the regulations had the effect of reducing the efficiency of the expeditions, so that with a quota of 15,000 B.W.U. they barely covered their costs, then clearly any appreciably lower quota would result in losses, unless efficiency could be increased.

Since allocation of a quota to countries or expeditions is specifically excluded from the Convention, discussions on this question took place outside the Convention. The first meeting was held in November, 1958. At this there was agreement that the Soviet share of the quota should be 20 per cent, but failure to agree on the division among the other countries (U.K., Norway, Japan, and Netherlands). The 20 per cent share for U.S.S.R. was rather more than double her share in the 1957/58 season, but was reached in the knowledge that the U.S.S.R. had under construction or planned several large new factory ships. The other countries presumably felt, correctly, that it was in their interests to accept some increase in Soviet catches, if in so doing the amount of the increase could be controlled.

It was more difficult to reach agreement on how the outstanding 80 per cent should be shared. As a result of the deadlock at the November, 1958, meeting, Norway, the Netherlands, and Japan successively gave notice of withdrawal from the Convention, stressing as they did so that they would cancel the notice if the allocation problem could be solved. Despite this form of mutual pressure negotiations dragged on for nearly four years, and the final agreement was not signed until June, 1962.

During the negotiations over the quota both Norway and the Netherlands, but not Japan, did withdraw from the Commission (on 30 June, 1959). Norway rejoined in 1960, but again gave notice of withdrawal at the end of 1961. This notice was cancelled, and the Netherlands rejoined in 1962, when the agreement on the division of the quota was reached. This withdrawal of two of the main whaling countries caused the breakdown of the formal arrangements for the conservation of the Antarctic whales. With the absence of Norway and the Netherlands the limit of 15,000 B.W.U. set by the schedule to the Convention, would apply only to Japan, U.K., and U.S.S.R. and could not act as any effective limit to their operations. The Commission therefore agreed to suspend the formal limit, and instead resolved that all countries should limit their catches to the amount taken in the 1959/60 season. This resolution was not followed exactly, but all countries set some limit on their catches, in accordance with their interpretation of this Resolution, and the state of the agreement on the division of the overall quota. Thus, for example, U.S.S.R. considered itself entitled to 20 per cent of the overall quota, and therefore took 20 per cent of the 1959/60 quota, i.e. 3000 B.W.U. As a result the catches in the 1960/61 and 1961/62 season were restricted, and the total catches were 16,433 and 15,252 B.W.U. respectively.

The agreement on quota allocation was only for a short period (the 1962 agreement as signed was only operative until the end of the 1965/66 season), and contained no provision for amendment of the shares. However, there was provision for a revision of the shares to allow for any transfer or sale of factory vessels from one country to another. Nominally the modification of the shares was only a minor consequence of the transfer of vessels, but as the total quota decreased, the number of available factory ships was far more than was required to harvest the quota. Sales of expeditions then had as their main purpose the transfer of the share of the quota. In some cases after expeditions were sold the vessels themselves were not moved, but laid up in the home ports of the vendor country.

In this way, there was an effective market for shares of Antarctic whaling. This market enabled Japan, with her developing industry (which had the advantage of both efficient and low cost operating and a valuable home market for whale meat), to increase her share, while the European countries (Netherlands and U.K., and to some extent Norway), could withdraw with profit. These transfers released most of the pressure for major renegotiations regarding the allocation. Discussions on the quota division have taken place regularly, but the original shares, as modified by subsequent transfers of expeditions, have not greatly changed, and the agreement has now lasted well past its original finishing date.

The beginning of the 1962/63 season, with a major cause of the economic difficulties of the industry solved for some years, should therefore have been the start of a more successful time for the Whaling Commission. Unfortunately the lengthy discussions over the quota allocation, plus the inability of the scientist to give clear and unanimous advice, had caused the Commission to fail in its primary task of maintaining the stocks at a good level. The blue whale stocks had been reduced to low level for a long time, and during the five years up to 1963 the fin whales too had been rapidly declining. The period immediately following 1963 was therefore the most difficult in the Commission's history. To understand these difficulties it is necessary to examine the population dynamics of the whale stocks in more detail.

THE SUSTAINABLE YIELD OF ANTARCTIC WHALES

The feature of the whale biology which dominates the possible pattern of sustainable yield is the low reproductive rate. An adult female can produce no more than one young every other year, so that the gross addition to the stock can be no more than 25 per cent of the number of adults, since the sex ratio is about an equal number of males and females. Because the rate of breeding is never quite as high as one calf every other year and because a fairly high proportion of young die before reaching maturity the gross additions to the mature stock of young animals maturing for the first time is considerably less than 25 per cent. (The stock of mature animals is not quite the same as the group of animals that is exposed to hunting, but the difference is not large.)

Subtracting from this gross recruitment the deaths due to causes other than fishing, gives the net rate of national increase. This is the rate at which the population would increase in the absence of fishing, or, viewed another way, it is the cropping rate which would leave the population unaltered, neither increasing nor decreasing. This sustainable rate must be less than the gross recruitment, and therefore *a fortiori* considerably less than the 25 per cent which is the upper limit of the reproductive rate. It appears, for moderately small stocks, to be in the region of 10 per cent or rather less (*see Fig.* 3 from Chapman, 1964). This curve, giving the relation between the sustainable yield and stock abundance, is that deduced for the blue whale stock. The points are values estimated for individual years. The estimation procedure, described in Chapman (1964), expressed the sustainable yield as the change in population abundance (derived from the catch per unit effort) plus the catch. Since the variability in catch per unit effort, as an index of abundance, is not small, the variance in the changes from year to year is high, and the individual points in *Fig.* 3, are highly scattered except at low population sizes.

However, if it is accepted that the population of blue whales was in equilibrium in 1910, the net natural rate of increase, i.e. the sustainable yield, then must have been zero. The unexploited population size is not easy to determine with very great precision. An extreme upper limit, given by the total of all whales killed since 1910, plus the few present survivors is about a third of a million, but a more realistic estimate is a little over 200,000, as shown in the diagram. Since the curve must cut the x-axis at this value of population, and at the origin, the plotted points, scattered though they are, suffice to determine the curve quite closely.

This curve, and the corresponding curves for the other stocks, supply the basic biological information required for management of the Antarctic stocks. From it the effect on the stock, and hence on the future catches, of any pattern of exploitation can be determined. For instance, the catches of blue whales in the post-war period could be plotted on the figure. During this period the catches exceeded the sustainable yield by a factor of around 3, and about 30 per cent of the stock was being taken each year. Thus the stock declined at about 20 per cent per year. Though the catches declined at around the same rate, the excess of catch over sustainable yield was maintained, and the decline continued until the blue whale was for commercial purposes extinct. The recognition of this extinction was delayed for a few seasons by the discovery in the southern Indian Ocean of a separate group of so-called pygmy blue whales, which supported a small

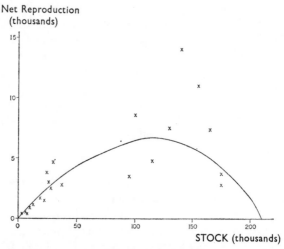

Fig. 3.—Net reproduction (sustainable yield) of blue whales, as a function of stock abundance. Points are estimates from individual seasons. (*Adapted from* Chapman, 1964.)

fishery, principally by Japanese expeditions, for a few seasons from 1960/61. At the fifteenth meeting of the I.W.C., in 1963, killing of blue whales in the Antarctic was prohibited except for a small area between 0° and 80° E.; at the 1964 meeting this prohibition was extended to the whole Antarctic. By then, the blue whale stocks were so depleted that, at an annual 10 per cent increase, it would take some fifty years to rebuild them (Chapman, 1964). Since catching of blue whales has been prohibited the best data on their abundance has ceased to be available; information is being collected on blue whales sighted by whaling ships (also by other ships, though identification of species may not be so good). This is not directly comparable with earlier, catch per unit effort data. It has not been collected over a long enough period, nor is the precision achieved high enough to determine whether or not the blue whale stock is recovering, and if so whether it is increasing at about 10 per cent per year. The results so far are at least not inconsistent with such an increase, and do suggest that in a few years a firmer conclusion will be reached. They also show that blue whales (and also right whales) are by no means extinct in the Antarctic, quite a number of both species being seen (Gulland, 1972).

The story of the blue whale stock in the post-war period is tragic, but basically simple. By 1945 the stock (around 30–40,000 animals) was well below the level giving the maximum yield, and decreases in abundance were reflected almost proportionally in decreases in sustainable yield. In this situation any decrease in abundance is clearly undesirable.

This is not always so. In an unexploited stock the net rate of increase is nil on the average, though there may be fluctuations. At these high levels of population the effective reproductive rate is reduced, or the natural mortality rate is increased, or both, so that addition to the stock of new recruits is equal to the losses by natural deaths. In the fin whale stock there is no direct evidence of changes in natural mortality (though these would be difficult to detect), but there have been observable changes both in the pregnancy rate, i.e. the proportion of the mature females that breed each year (Laws, 1962), and in the age at which they become mature (around ten years in the unexploited stock, but as low as five years in the present heavily exploited stock—Lockyer, 1972). These observed differences are sufficient to allow recruitment and natural mortality to be in balance in an unexploited population; but for there to be an excess of recruitment over natural deaths of around 10 per cent of the adult stock in a heavily exploited population (Gulland, 1971).

The greatest yield (the maximum in *Fig.* 3) can be taken at some moderate population size, where both the net rate of increase, as a percentage of the population, and the population size itself, are moderately high.

It is therefore desirable, from the point of view of obtaining a large yield, to reduce the population if it is much above the level giving this maximum. Immediately after the war the fin whale stock was probably around this optimum level, or possibly even above it, while the sei whale stock was unexploited. Therefore, a decrease in the sei whale stocks (and possibly also the fin whale stock) was not necessarily a bad thing.

Immediately after the war the fin whale stock, in addition to being near its optimum abundance, was probably being harvested at close to the optimum rate. The maximum sustainable yield was estimated by the Committee of Three Scientists as 20,000 animals (Chapman, 1964), though more recent studies suggest that this is rather too high. The annual pelagic catch between 1946 and 1951 was also about 20,000. After 1951, as the blue whales stock and catches declined, without any change in overall quota (in B.W.U.) the total catches of fin whales increased to around 28,000 from 1954–62, about 25,000 of which was taken by pelagic expeditions. The stock therefore declined, at first by around 8000 per year, but as the decline in abundance continued, the sustainable yield also began to decrease. At first the sustainable yield fell, slowly, but as it fell progressively further below 20,000, the gap between it and the actual catch widened, and the decrease of both stock and sustainable yield accelerated. By 1964 the fin whale stock was in a similar state to that of the blue whale stock of a decade or so earlier.

With the whole history of Antarctic whaling before us, and also with improved theoretical models, it is easy to understand what happened to the fin whales, and to deplore the missed opportunities in the 1950s, when the fin whale stocks at least could have been stabilized at a productive level. The picture at that time was not so clear. For some time the changes in the abundance were not large, and these were difficult to detect. The best estimate of abundance came from the catch per unit effort, and this was distorted by many factors, especially changes in the efficiency of individual catchers, and by the switch in attention from blue whales to fin whales. There was therefore considerable uncertainty among some scientists as to what the precise state of the fin whale stock was. This uncertainty was in turn the cause, or at least the excuse, for the failure of the Commission to take action while such action would have been relatively painless, i.e. when the reduction in the quota necessary to reduce the fin whale catches to no more than the stock could withstand was only a moderate proportion of the total quota. By the time the report of the Special Committee of Three Scientists put the facts of the situation clearly before the Commission, the reduction required was of the order of 70 per cent—from 25,000 whales to 7000. Such a reduction was too great for the whaling industry (and indeed for any industry) to accept immediately. In the few years it took to be accepted, the situation became still worse.

The first clear move to reduce the quota as a protection for fin whales occurred at the Commission's Seventh meeting, in

Moscow in 1955. At that time it had before it a very clear report from the scientists. This pointed out that the catches of this species had increased from 17,474 in 1950/51 to nearly 26,000 in 1954/55, that this higher level of catch seemed to be resulting in a decrease in the stock, and that to maintain what had become commercially the most important species in the Antarctic, catches should be reduced to something like the former level. A figure of 19,000 was suggested. The 1500 blue whales, which was believed to be the catch currently obtainable, plus some humpback and sei whales would have implied a B.W.U. quota of 11,500–12,000, against the quota for the 1954/55 season of 15,500 B.W.U.

Though the 1955 scientific report contained this clear indication of what should be done, it also contained signs of the two weaknesses which were to become more pronounced and almost fatal to the Commission. These were a reluctance to give the Commission unpleasant advice, and a disagreement among the scientists, expressed as reservations on the part of one of the Dutch scientists.

While the scientific sub-committee (as it then was) clearly believed (or most of it believed) that the quota should be, if the stock were to be maintained, no more than 12,000 B.W.U., they also recognized that an immediate reduction from 15,500 B.W.U. would be highly unpopular with the whaling industries. Rather than leave the decision on the balance between long- and short-term interests to the Commission, or even better describing the long- and short-term results of possible courses of action, the scientists themselves suggested a compromise, of 14,500 B.W.U. for the 1955/56 season.

Not surprisingly, the Commission took advantage of this suggestion, but in general treated the figure of 14,500 more as an ultimate objective rather than an interim measure. Small though the suggested reduction was, it was unacceptable to some countries, and the recommendation that was finally agreed (by an 11–3 majority) was for a reduction in two stages, to 15,000 in the 1955/56 season, and to 14,500 thereafter. Even then, the second part was formally objected to by the Netherlands, and subsequently by other countries. At subsequent meetings new recommendations to lower the quota were made, against the arguments of the Netherlands and others, and a quota of 14,500 units was in force for 1956/57 and 1957/58, but a further extension was formally objected to, and the quota reverted to 15,000 B.W.U., where it remained until 1963.

Subsequent years saw little change in the situation. The scientists continued to point out, with increasing conviction except for one or two dissenters, that the fin whale stocks were decreasing, and that the quota should be reduced. The Commission continued to be divided (with about the same national division as the scientists) on the need for such reduction and also was deeply involved with the question of the national allocation of quotas. The decisive action on the first of these deadlocks was taken at the Twelfth meeting, in 1960, when a special committee of three scientists was appointed.

This Committee of Three (D. G. Chapman from the U.S.A., S. J. Holt from F.A.O., and K. R. Allen, then working in New Zealand), which subsequently became a Committee of Four with the addition of J. A. Gulland from the U.K., was appointed on the basis of their individual expertise in population dynamics, without reference to knowledge of whales. In fact, it was an initial condition that the members should not be drawn from countries actively engaged in Antarctic pelagic whaling. The Commission, in setting up the Committee, also made the important declaration that it had the intention of bringing, not later than 31 July, 1964, the Antarctic catch limit into line with the scientific findings, having regard to the provisions of paragraph 2 of Article V of the Convention. This referred to item (d) of that paragraph that regulations should take into consideration the interests of the consumers of whale products and the whaling industry. The Convention does not say anything about the possible conflict between long- and short-term interests, or between those of consumers and producers. In effect, this paragraph was interpreted to protect the short-term interests of the producers.

The Committee of Three presented its final report to the Commission in 1963. This set out very clearly the state of the stocks, and has been the basis of all later studies of the Antarctic stocks. To do this the well-established techniques used to study the population dynamics of fishes were adapted to the similar but distinct problems of whales. This enabled many of the points of disagreement among the whale scientists (who were not specialists in these techniques) to be cleared up.

More important, the Commission was given a simple and comprehensible theoretical framework—the concept of the sustainable yield, and in essence the form of the curve shown in *Fig.* 3—against which it could judge the effectiveness and practical consequences of its decisions. In addition to the stick of warnings of declining stocks it was also given the carrot of catches continuing at a moderately high level, once the stocks had been established at their optimum level.

After the disagreements among their previous advisers, and its decision to seek other advice, the Commission was no doubt disposed to accept as reliable the report of the Committee of Three, but this acceptance was helped by the results of the 1963/64 season. As described later, attempts to reduce the quota, on the basis of the new advice were only partly successful, and the quota for that season was reduced from 15,000 B.W.U., but only as far as 10,000 B.W.U. With due allowance for a few blue whales taken in the pygmy blue whale area, and some sei whales, to reach such a quota would have required catching some 17–18,000 fin whales. It was pointed out that if the catching effort remained the same as in 1962/63 (as it was likely to do, since virtually all the ships involved would be the same), the catch in 1963/64 would only be 14,000 fin whales. Far from acting as an additional restriction on the level of catching effort, the new revised quota could not in fact be reached. The events of 1963/64 bore out the prediction—superficially almost exactly. The actual pelagic catch was 13,870 fin whales—only 130 different from the predicted figure, and several thousands below what the industry had hoped for when the quota had been set.

Subsequent analysis has shown that such close agreement, within 1 per cent, was a matter of luck. Unpredictable variations, e.g. in the weather, cause annual variations in catch per unit effort of the order of 5 per cent; further, an almost equally good prediction could have been obtained by direct extrapolation of the existing trend in catch per unit. However, the agreement occurred, and this greatly helped the acceptance of the scientific validity of the Committee of Three's report. It did not, unfortunately, make it much easier for the Commission to act on the report.

In 1955 the difference between the fin whale catch, including both pelagic expeditions and shore stations, and the sustainable yield was, as noted above, only a few thousand (c. 28,000 against 20,000), and a reduction of catch to bring it into line with the sustainable yield, though doubtless unpleasant for the industry, could not be considered as so drastic as to be against that part of the Convention which invokes the interest of the whaling industry. By 1963 the sustainable yield had fallen to an estimated 4800 fin whales (supplementary report of the Committee of Three, in Fourteenth Report of the I.W.C.). An immediate limit of catches of fin whales to no more than the sustainable yield therefore required that the catches of the most important species of whale should be reduced, in comparison with the 1962/63 catches, by 75 per cent. This was far more than the whaling industry—with no immediate alternative employment for the vessels, and in the case of Norway, with whole communities very largely dependant on whaling—could stand.

In 1963 and 1964 the Commission had a series of critical meetings, with a clear split between those—mainly the countries which were not actively engaged in Antarctic whaling—who wanted the quota reduced as quickly as possible to at most the level agreed to be the combined current sustainable yields of each species, and those—the countries with large industries dependant on Antarctic whaling—who would like to maintain the quota at a high level. At the Fifteenth meeting in 1963 the gap was very wide, between a proposal for the 1963/64 season of 4000 B.W.U. on one side, and 10,000 or 12,000 B.W.U. on the other. The figure of 10,000 was adopted, and accepted by those favouring a lower quota, because they realized that if a lower quota was insisted on, against the wishes of several active whaling countries, they would object within the statutory ninety days, and the quota would revert to 15,000 B.W.U. This was perhaps wrong tactics, because the stocks were so depleted that even the 10,000 B.W.U. quota could not be reached by the current fleets, as shown by the failure to catch more than 14,000 fin whales.

These tactics were not repeated at the 1964 meeting, where the gap was as wide as ever. The conservation proposal was for a phased reduction, of quotas of 4000, 3000, and 2000 B.W.U. in the seasons from 1964/65 to 1966/67. The counter-proposal was for 8500 B.W.U. (by Japan and U.S.S.R.) or 6000 B.W.U. (by Norway). No proposal obtained the necessary two-thirds majority, and no recommendation was made by the Commission. The Antarctic countries met among themselves, and agreed a figure of 8000 B.W.U. for the 1964/65 season, but only just under 7000 B.W.U. were taken.

Following this failure to reach agreement, it was clear that the Commission could not continue unless something more effective was done. A number of approaches were made to the whaling countries, by the members of the Commission, by various international organizations, especially those concerned with nature conservation, and by individuals. These approaches were helped by the adverse publicity that the Commission and its activities were receiving in the world's press, and by the realization that whale conservation was not just a matter that concerned a small exclusive club of a handful of countries.

Following these discussions, the final attempt to make the Commission fulfil its obligations took the form of a special meeting of the Commission. This was held in London in May, 1965, and after protracted discussions agreed to a proposal of 4500 B.W.U. for the 1965/66 season, and further reductions for the 1966/67 and 1967/68 seasons, such that the latter would be less than the combined sustainable yield of fin and sei whales (then estimated to be 4000 and 3000 whales respectively, or a total of 2500 B.W.U., though the estimate for sei whales was very rough).

A feature of the background scientific material for these meetings was the detailed studies of the comparative effects of different patterns of quotas (*see Table* 2).

Table 2.—The Effect of Various Quota Schemes on Fin Whale Catches (*from* I.W.C., 1966).

Proposal	Stock at beginning of 1968/69 Season	Sustainable Yield after 1967/68	Total Catch 1964/65– 1967/68
a. 4500, 4000, 3500 B.W.U.	33,700	4,100	15,300
b. 4000, 3000, 2000 B.W.U.	37,500	4,500	11,500
c. Effort half that in 1964/65	37,400	4,500	11,600
d. 3000, 2000, 2000 B.W.U.	40,000	4,800	9,000

These calculations enabled the Commission to make better judgements of the desirability of various actions, and were much more useful than some of the previous scientific reports. For instance, when these stated that the quota should be reduced, the reply from the whaling countries was, in effect, that from their point of view the quota should not be reduced. The detailed exposition of the consequences could make it clear that this argument was wrong.

At this time the Commission and the active whaling countries had one of their few pieces of good luck. This was the discovery of the sei whales stock as a valuable alternative to the depleted fin whales. Small, but generally increasing, numbers of sei whales had been taken for a long time, and they were included in the original B.W.U. formulation, six sei whales equalling one B.W.U. This equivalence was based on the relative yield of oils. In the 1960s the whaling companies, led by the Japanese, found more and more use for whale meat and meat by-products. The yield of meat from six sei whales was more than that from two fin whales (or one blue whale), so that, with the allocation of quotas, which removed the need to rush to catch as many whales as possible while the season lasted, sei whales became the most attractive species. Concentration of sei whales was found in waters north of the traditional Antarctic grounds, first in the south-west Antarctic (in the 1964/65 season) and in later years farther eastward. Catches of sei whales shot up from some 5000 in 1962/63 to 8000 in 1963/64 and nearly 20,000 in 1964/65.

These increased sei whale catches implied, within a given B.W.U. quota, correspondingly smaller fin whale catches. Although the 1964/65 quota was much more than was believed necessary by the scientists to bring catches down to the sustainable yield, the actual pelagic catch of fin whales in that season (4211 animals) was almost exactly equal to the sustainable yield of that species.

Without the sei whales, the delay in bringing down the quota to a proper level might have been as fatal as the similar failure had been, almost literally, to the blue whales. By 1967 excess catches in the intervening season might have reduced the sustainable yield well below the figure of 4000 or so whales that the whaling countries had brought themselves to accept, and further delay would have occurred, with even further decline in stocks, and so on, until the whales were commercially extinct. As it was, the excess catches were absorbed by the sei whales. Between 1964 and 1968 the total abundance of Antarctic sei whales was almost halved, to between 50,000 and 60,000 animals, and this level was not far from that giving the maximum sustainable yield (F.A.O. report in the Nineteenth I.W.C. Report). Thus it was possible to fulfil the obligation made in 1965, and bring the 1967/68 quota down to within the range of estimates of the combined sustainable yield.

SUSTAINABLE YIELD

Since 1967 the situation in Antarctic whaling has not changed greatly. The quota is low enough for the stocks to be further depleted at only a very slow rate, if at all, but no provision is being made for rebuilding the fin whale stocks at any significant rate. There is also the worry that the Commission has tended to take the higher value of sustainable yield within the range suggested by the scientists. If the lower values are the true ones, the stocks are in fact still declining slowly. Further, there was until 1972 no provision for separate regulations for different stocks, though the present division between species is probably not far from the optimum.

The activities of the whaling industry and of the I.W.C. attracted little public attention around 1964, when the situation was critical and the future of the Commission, of the whaling industry, and of the whales themselves were very much in balance. This lack of attention was reversed in 1971 and 1972, when whales, in common with other marine mammals, received very great attention from conservation interests, particularly in the United States. This interest culminated at the United Nations Conference on the Human Environment at Stockholm in June, 1972. At this Conference a resolution was passed, by a very large majority, proposing a ten-year moratorium on the killing of all whales. All those without whaling industries voted for the moratorium, and virtually all those with whaling interests abstained—a vote which, on both sides, can be viewed with some degree of cynicism.

The scientific basis of the proposal has been unclear. On the one hand, those species of whales—blue, humpback, grey, and right—which are in possible danger of extinction, had been fully protected by the I.W.C. for some time. Although doubts can, and are, expressed concerning the full effectiveness of the I.W.C. recommendations, similar doubts could be expressed, with even greater force, concerning the effect of a resolution from the Human Environment Conference. Also a fixed-term moratorium, with the implication that whaling would be permissible after that time, could have serious consequences for such species as blue whales, for which a much longer period of complete protection is desirable.

On the other hand, other stocks of whales, such as sei and sperm whales, are probably not far from the optimum level, i.e. the abundance at which the maximum sustained yield can be taken. There seems no justification for stopping catching these whales— at least from the management point of view. There is another viewpoint, on which any killing of marine mammals is inhumane, and should not be permitted, despite the loss of the production of oil and meat involved. Though an understandable viewpoint, it is irrelevant to the question of whether or not the whale stocks are being properly managed. From this latter aspect there is no doubt that a moratorium on hunting of sei whales would be undesirable, since it would lead to an immediate loss of production, which could not be made up by intensified harvesting after the end of the moratorium.

The question of a moratorium was also considered by the International Whaling Commission at its session in London which immediately followed the Stockholm conference. Not surprisingly, the proposal to implement a general moratorium for all whale species was rejected. However, the general public outcry and dissatisfaction with the I.W.C. (in fact justified more by its record in 1964 than in 1972) did have some good effects. The Antarctic quotas were, as already agreed in principle at the 1971 I.W.C. session, expressed separately for each species, rather than in Blue Whale Units. Also the quota for fin whales for the 1972/73 Antarctic season was set at a figure—2000 animals—below the best estimates of the sustainable yield, and also well below both recent catches, and the figure previously used in calculating the total, B.W.U., quota in earlier seasons. For example, the 1971/72 season's quota was 2300 B.W.U., calculated as about 2700 fin whales plus 5700 sei whales.

In addition, it seems that the pressure of world public opinion will ensure that at last the International Observer Scheme, under which observers for other whaling countries are carried on board factory ships, or attached to shore stations, and which has been agreed in principle for several years, will come into operation.

These changes, though less significant than the drastic cuts in quotas agreed in the 1960s, and particularly the achievements of the critical Special Meeting in May, 1965, do represent further progress in the rational management of the whale stocks. Though opportunities have been missed, notably of ensuring that the blue whales make a further contribution to catches in the present century, Antarctic whales are now being managed in a reasonable and rational manner, and should contribute increasingly to the world food supply.

REFERENCES

CHAPMAN, D. G. (1964), 'Reports of the Committee of Three Scientists on the Special Scientific Investigation of the Antarctic Whale Stocks', *Rep. int. Comm. Whal.*, **14,** 32–106.

GULLAND, J. A. (1971), 'The effect of exploitation on the numbers of marine animals', *Proc. Adv. Study Inst. Dynamics Numbers Popul.* (Oosterbeck, 1970), 450–468.

GULLAND, J. A. (1972), 'Future of the blue whale', *New Scientist*, **54,** 198–199.

LAWS, R. M. (1959), 'Age determination of whales by means of corpora albicantia', *Proc. XVth int. Congr. Zool.*, 303–5.

LAWS, R. M. (1962), 'Some effects of whaling on the southern stocks of baleen whales', in *The Exploitation of Natural Animal Populations* (ed. Le Cren and Holdgate), 137–58. Oxford: Blackwell.

LOCKYER, C. (1972), 'The age at sexual maturity of the southern fin whale (*Balaenoptera physalus*) using annual layer counts in the ear plug', *J. Cons. int. Explor. Mer*, **34** (2), 276–294.

MACKINTOSH, N. A. (1965), *Stocks of Whales*, 232. London: Fishing News (Books) Ltd.

OHSUMI, S. (1964), 'Examination on age determination of the fin whale', *Sci. Rep. Whales Res. Inst., Tokyo*, **18,** 49–88.

Chapter

3

NORTH ATLANTIC TRAWL FISHERIES

THE trawl is, with the purse seine, the most efficient device for harvesting fish so far devised. Its efficiency has been the immediate cause of most of the problems of fishery management arising in the world today. These problems are therefore well illustrated by the history of trawling in its home ground, which is the North Atlantic, and more particularly the North Sea. The North Atlantic fisheries are both the oldest and the most complex in the world, and for simplicity discussion will be limited to the area and stocks covered by the present-day English demersal ('white fish') fishery. Even this includes a vast area, from Ushant in the south to Spitsbergen in the north, and from northern Russia westward to New England. This covers an area of some $3\frac{1}{2}$ million km² of shelf—waters of depth less than 200 m.—or about one-fifth of the world total. The most northern parts of the area are cold, and covered with ice for much of the year. In much of the rest of the area the mixture of waters—the warm water of the Gulf stream and its extensions moving north and westward, and the cold waters from the Arctic—provide a rich bloom of plants, the animals that feed on them, and so on along the food chain to man. There are also wide areas of shallow shelf —the Grand Banks of Newfoundland, the North Sea, and the Barents Sea. This fortunate combination of suitable topography and high biological production supports large populations of bottom-living fish, and make much of the North Atlantic among the richest fishing grounds of the world.

This is the kingdom of the cod. Over most of the northern part of the area it is by far the commonest commercial bottom-living fish—so does it dominate the fisheries that often 'fish', without further description, means cod, only the lesser varieties, such as haddock or redfish needing further specification (Innis, 1954;

Graham, 1948). The potential annual catch of cod is of the order of $3\frac{1}{2}$-4 million tons (Gulland, 1972), and recent catches have approached this level. The value of the catch in 1971, though not known precisely, was probably around U.S. $500 million. According to the joint working group of biologists and economists set up by the International Commission for the North-west Atlantic Fisheries (I.C.N.A.F.) the effort expended in taking this catch could be reduced by 20 per cent without affecting the catch. The prize for managing this stock is therefore at least $100 million per year.

The cod do not move freely throughout the area, but form a number of more or less discrete stocks (*Fig.* 4); the biggest ones are in the North-east Arctic (between northern Norway, Russia, and Spitsbergen), at Iceland, off West Greenland, off Labrador and northern Newfoundland, and on the Grand Banks, though there are a number of smaller, but still important stocks, such as those in the North Sea, and off Nova Scotia. *Table* 3 shows the catches from the more important stocks during recent years. In all areas the cod grows to about the same size: a big cod is some 100–120 cm. long, weighing perhaps 15 kg., and the occasional fish even bigger. However, many of the fish caught are of much smaller size, in the range 50–60 cm., and often even smaller, weighing only 1 kg. or less.

It is this difference between the size of fish that are caught and the size they might reach if allowed to grow which provides one of the needs, or opportunities, for effective management. While the cod reaches much the same size in all areas, the growth is much faster in the warmer, southern areas (*see* papers of the symposium on cod, I.C.E.S., 1954). The fastest growing cod are those to the south of Ireland, which may reach 50 cm. at the end of the second year of life, and 90 cm. in four years; at the other extreme, a 50-cm. cod at Labrador may be as much as ten years old.

Even in the northern areas, cod is not the only fish in the sea or even the only bottom-living fish, and species such as redfish, catfish (wolffish), and halibut make welcome additions to the catch of cod trawlers, or support fisheries in their own right. Farther south, in the North Sea, or off New England, there is a much greater variety of species. A Lowestoft trawler fishing in the North Sea may, in the same trip, or even in the same haul, catch a dozen or more species, principally cod, plaice, haddock, or sole, but often also useful quantities of other flatfish, such as turbot, brill, or lemon sole, and others, such as whiting or skates.

Table 3.—Annual Average Catches of Cod (thousand tons) 1966–70, from Major North Atlantic Stocks (Data from I.C.E.S./I.C.N.A.F. Cod Working Group report.)

Stock	North-East Arctic	Iceland	S.W. East Greenland	West Greenland	Labrador North Newfoundland	Grand Banks	S.W. Newfoundland	Nova Scotia	Other N.E. Atlantic	Other N.W. Atlantic
Canada	—	—	—	—	113	5	29	52	—	96
Denmark	10	3	23	44	15	—	—	—	108	2
France	+	+	3	29	60	1	4	1	32	29
Germany (F.R.)	5	20	48	59	58	—	—	+	38	+
Iceland	—	247	7	+	+	+	—	—	+	+
Netherlands	+	+	—	—	—	—	—	—	25	—
Norway	272	+	8	25	21	1	—	+	7	—
Poland	1	—	+	+	59	6	+	+	64	2
Portugal	—	—	3	36	126	68	+	1	—	18
Spain	—	—	1	14	101	—	27	5	+	64
Sweden	—	—	—	—	—	—	—	—	27	—
U.K.	148	117	5	6	21	1	1	+	121	3
U.S.A.	—	—	—	—	—	—	—	+	—	21
U.S.S.R.	399	1	+	1	89	59	4	+	52	13
Others	—	—	4	9	47	1	+	+	2	+
Total	835	391	102	223	710	142	65	60	476	248

Note: + denotes an average annual catch of less than 1000 tons;
— denotes no catch from the stock.

THE FISHERIES

The start of fishing around the coasts of the North Atlantic is lost in pre-history. Important fishing industries are centuries old. Fishermen from England, France, and elsewhere were going to Iceland in the fifteenth century and earlier, catching cod on hand-lines and salting the fish. They were only a few years behind Columbus and Cabot in discovering the riches of the new world, especially the waters around Newfoundland (Morison, 1971; Innis, 1954). The last survivors of these fisheries are the dory fishermen of Portugal. These still put out, each man in his own small boat, from the mothership—mostly motor vessels, though there are a few remaining schooners—to jig for cod with hand-lines, returning at the end of each day to split and salt the catch.

While this old way of fishing still survives, as does the almost equally old inshore fisheries, using cod traps and other gear along the Newfoundland and Labrador coasts, the modern age of fishing, with its increased catches and increased problems, comes from the application of the technology of the industrial revolution to fishing. Above all this has involved the development of the steam (later motor) trawler, though the initial rise of trawling in the middle of the nineteenth century was due to the new railways and the manufacture of ice, which allowed fresh fish to be delivered to a much wider market. It was not until 1875 that the steam trawler was introduced. Largely based on the Humber ports of Grimsby and Hull, which were to be the centres of English trawling for the next century, the English fleet soon spread over most of the North Sea (Alward, 1932). Although English trawler-men led the way in the development of North Sea trawling, other countries were not slow in following. In the inter-war period and later, these countries, particularly Germany, were active leaders in the spread of trawling to more distant ground.

Before the end of the century it was clear that the North Sea was heavily fished. The total catch had ceased to increase, and the catch per boat had fallen sharply. The English trawler owners were therefore looking farther afield for new supplies. Plaice keeps better on ice than does cod, and fetches a higher price than cod, and so became the first objective of the longer trawl voyages, both to Iceland, and also to the so-called White Sea—actually the North Russian coast, north of the enclosed waters of the true White Sea—to which the first voyages were made in 1906 (Atkinson, 1908). By 1914 falling plaice stocks, and increasing attention to haddock and cod, meant that plaice accounted for only 5 per cent of the total English annual landings from Iceland of 80,000–100,000 tons, compared with about 50 per cent cod and 20 per cent haddock.

The outbreak of war in 1914 brought a sharp end to much of the fishing in the North-east Atlantic. Most of the North Sea and adjacent waters were not very safe to fish in, and many of the fishing boats were pressed into naval service. By 1918 the stocks had benefited from four years without fishing, and were more abundant than for half a century. The post-war increase in stocks showed clearly that the shortage of fish in the North Sea was due to heavy fishing, rather than to some natural fluctuation, but the recovery was short lived. Good catches in the immediate post-war years resulted in a rush of new construction, which on top of the ships built for patrol service or minesweeping during the war, and which made admirable trawlers, resulted in an over-capacity in ships which was to cripple the economy of the English North Sea trawl fishery for the next thirty years. The difficulties of the North Sea fleet started as soon as the high post-war stock levels declined in the early 1920s, but became more pronounced with the general economic depression of the 1930s.

By the mid 1920s, therefore, interest had again turned to the more distant grounds. While the plaice stocks at Iceland and in the Barents Sea had already become fully exploited in the decade before the first world war, and the haddock stocks were not much larger, and were becoming heavily exploited, the great stocks of cod at Iceland, and around Bear Island and in the Barents Sea allowed a continual increase in catches during the 1920s and 1930s. This increase was mainly due to the growing trawling on the immature fish, particularly by English vessels, though also Germany and other countries took an important share. It was additional to the important and long-established local fisheries on spawning and pre-spawning fish in south-west Iceland, and around the Lofoten Islands in northern Norway. By 1939 the total catches of cod from the Arcto–Norwegian stock—the fish which spawn at the Lofoten Islands, and have their feeding grounds in the Barents Sea and around Bear Island—were approaching a million tons; catches at Iceland had reached a peak of half a million tons in 1933, with a decline in the following years due more to natural causes (year-class fluctuations) than to fishing. The amount of fishing on these stocks was approaching, or might even have passed, the optimum level, but not for so long, or to such a marked extent, as to compel some reaction from the fishery —such as a move to new grounds, or the introduction of significant measures for the management and conservation of the stocks.

The second world war then intervened, and had the same beneficial effects, though over a wider area, as the first war, dispersing

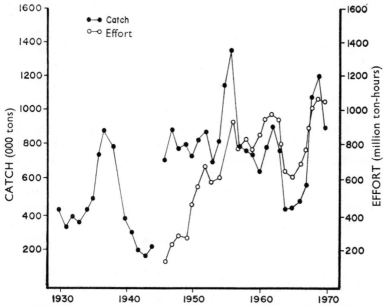

Fig. 5.—Trends in catches (full circles) and fishing effort (open circles) of cod in the North-east Arctic. Note little change in catch from 1947 onwards, despite increasing effort. (*Data from* I.C.E.S. reports.)

any doubts there might be that heavy fishing resulted in a shortage of fish. After the war fishing developments at first were a continuation of the pre-war policies, with the English owners building each year slightly larger and faster vessels (but in essence no different from the 1920 trawler) so as to bring back yet larger catches of 'fresh' cod stowed in bulk on ice for the fish-and-chip trade. A new element was the increasing participation of Russian, and later other eastern European countries. While neither the English nor the German or Norwegian effort in the Barents Sea increased much beyond their pre-war levels, the increasing Russian effort soon raised the total amount of fishing beyond the pre-war level, and resulted in the classic signs of falling catch rates (catch per boat), and a stable or even falling total catch despite increasing fishing (*Fig.* 5).

The ensuing search for new grounds was helped by a major technical innovation—the freezing of fish on board a trawler at sea. This greatly increased the distance from home at which a ship could operate and still bring back fresh fish. Sea-frozen fish may not be the same as fish straight out of the sea, but is much closer to it than fish that has been sitting on ice for two weeks. Freezing was soon combined with another important change— hauling the trawl over a stern ramp, with the ship heading into the sea, rather than working it over the side, with the ship beam on to the sea. Stern trawling is more comfortable for the crew, and can be done in worse weather. The combination of freezing and stern trawling gave rise to the self-contained factory trawler; though pioneered by the British Fairtry, built twenty years ago, the idea has been adopted by many other countries, particularly the Russians, whose series of Tropik and Atlantic class vessels are common sights in all the oceans of the world.

The depletion of the Barents Sea initiated, and the freezer trawler aided, the last great spread of North Atlantic bottom fishing into those parts of the North-west Atlantic—off West Greenland, Labrador, and some areas and stocks farther south— which were still lightly exploited. In 1950 the salt cod was still, as it had been for four centuries, the main feature of the North-west Atlantic fisheries. In the North-west Atlantic the only real equivalent to the heavily fished North Sea and Icelandic stocks was the New England fishery for haddock on Georges Bank which had become fully exploited in the 1930s (Graham, 1954), and a few other minor fisheries.

The twenty years from 1950 saw a transformation of the fisheries in the North-west Atlantic, and doubling of the catches. In 1950 barely one-third of the total catch was taken by vessels from outside North America, but by 1970 the proportion had risen to nearly two-thirds. In 1950 the long-range fleets were almost wholly the traditional salt cod fleets of Spain, France, Portugal, and Italy, but these have barely maintained their catches. Italy in fact has stopped fishing in the North-west Atlantic. The big increase in long-distance fishing has been the freezer-trawler from U.S.S.R., Poland, and both Germanies. In addition to increasing the pressure on the traditional stocks, such as the cod on the Grand Banks, they have spread their attention to all other major cod stocks, such as those off Labrador, which had previously been only lightly exploited, and to other species, such as silver hake. The flexibility of the operations of these long-range fleets, partly aided by the central planning and control of the eastern European fleets, allowed catches from individual stocks to expand very quickly. Once the possibilities of fishing on a particular stock had been established, dozens or even hundreds of ships could be concentrated on it. For example, catches of cod off Labrador went up from 60 thousand tons in 1959 to over a quarter of a million tons in 1961; and off Nova Scotia silver hake catches increased from 9 thousand tons in 1962 to 123 thousand tons in 1963.

The local North American fisheries have also changed. Though in Newfoundland and Labrador much of the catch is still taken by small boats close inshore, using a variety of gear such as cod traps, with the catch being salted, an increasing part of the Canadian catch is taken by modern side and stern trawlers supplying freezing plants.

Table 4 shows the distribution of catches in 1970, by each country in the main areas of the North-west Atlantic. This table shows that a number of countries fish in each area, but also shows that even the long-range fleets do not spread evenly over the whole region, and that each country tends to have its favoured grounds. Also while some countries, such as France and Portugal, continue to fish almost entirely for cod, the newer countries, such as the U.S.S.R., are less particular, only concentrating on cod in the northern areas, such as off Labrador.

While the main thrust of European demersal fishing since the war has been in the construction of large long-range fleets, working to a large extent outside European waters—apart from their interests in North-west Atlantic, Russia and Spain in particular have developed large fisheries in the southern Atlantic—the post-war period also saw important changes in the North Sea. By 1950 the steam trawlers built at the beginning of the century and up to 1920 were at last being scrapped in sufficient numbers to bring the capacity of the fleets into line with the productivity of the stocks. Though a couple of hundred British trawlers were built for North Sea fishing between 1950 and 1960, compared with less than half a dozen between 1920 and 1950, this barely compensated for the removal of the hundreds of old vessels, and the British North Sea effort was less than in the pre-war period. There was

Table 4.—TOTAL CATCHES (thousand tons) IN THE NORTH-WEST ATLANTIC BY I.C.N.A.F. MEMBER COUNTRIES IN 1970.
(In parentheses, catches of cod.)

REGION / I.C.N.A.F. AREA	GREENLAND 1	LABRADOR 2	N.E. NEWFOUNDLAND 3 KLM	GRAND BANKS 3 NOP	GULF OF ST. LAWRENCE 4 RST	NOVA SCOTIA 4 VWX	NEW ENGLAND 5
Canada (Maritimes and Quebec)	—	— (—)	5 (2)	19 (4)	338 (60)	288 (42)	47 (3)
Canada (Newfoundland)	—	3 (2)	158 (87)	221 (35)	81 (27)	7 (1)	—
Faroes (a)	8 (8)	+ (+)	—	10 (2)	—	8 (8)	—
Greenland	37 (20)	—					—
France	5 (5)	16 (16)	12 (12)	+	31 (31)	3 (3)	—
St. Pierre	—	—	1 (+)	5 (2)	+ (+)	+ (+)	—
Germany (F.R.)	45 (41)	51 (50)	12 (12)	—	—	6 (+)	92 (+)
Japan	—	—	2 (+)	2 (+)	—	5 (+)	11 (+)
Norway (a)	7 (6)	3 (3)	1 (1)	36 (35)	—	—	—
Poland	— (—)	41 (36)	26 (13)	+ (+)	—	2 (+)	102 (+)
Portugal	9 (9)	42 (42)	87 (87)	3 (3)	18 (18)	3 (3)	—
Romania	—	5 (3)	1 (+)	2 (+)	—	+ (—)	3 (+)
Spain	19 (19)	11 (11)	62 (6)	106 (103)	8 (8)	61 (58)	8 (7)
U.S.S.R.	8 (1)	65 (50)	80 (29)	106 (31)	—	284 (3)	166 (+)
U.K.	4 (3)	3 (3)	1 (1)	+ (+)	—	—	—
U.S.A.	—	+ (+)	+ (+)	— (—)	8 (+)	6 (1)	357 (22)
Total	141 (111)	239 (217)	448 (306)	511 (222)	485 (144)	673 (119)	687 (49)

Note: (a) Catches from sub-area 3 assumed to be from Grand Banks, and from sub-area 4 from Nova Scotia.
+ Catches less than 500 tons.
− Zero catch.

46

some increase in foreign fishing, but these countries too had found more interest in other stocks—distant water fishing, or herring, either for human consumption or for reduction to meal and oil, or in other fish (sand-eels or Norway pout) also for reduction purposes.

Another important change in the North Sea fishery has been the growth of Danish seining. This has taken two forms, anchor seining, principally for plaice, and practised predominantly by the Danes, and fly-dragging for round fish, such as haddock and whiting, mainly carried out by Scottish fishermen. In fly-dragging, the fish caught are much the same size as those in a trawl, but anchor-seining seems to catch rather bigger fish. The change-over to seining, which occurred in Denmark at about the beginning of the war, therefore resulted in an appreciable increase in the average size of plaice caught. This change, and the comparatively low level of effort has meant that the North Sea demersal stocks are in a more healthy state today than they have been in the past century (war-time effects excepted), in sharp contrast to many of the stocks in more distant water.

SCIENTIFIC RESEARCH

Just as the North Sea was the cradle of modern trawling, it has also been the cradle of much fishery research, especially that dealing with the quantitative studies of the effects of fishing on the stocks, in which British scientists have always played a leading part. The scientific investigations of the fisheries started toward the end of the nineteenth century, when it became clear that all was not well either with the fish stocks, or with the fisheries on them. This was approached by the usual British fashion of establishing a Royal Commission, in 1866 (and also further Commissions of Inquiry at intervals in later years). Its report, laid before Parliament in 1874, gave clear evidence of declining catch rates, and presumptive evidence that this was due to fishing. It also showed that lack of accurate past statistics of the fishery, and of knowledge of the basic biology of the fish, made precise conclusions difficult. As a result the collection of good statistical data was started.

Similar complaints and corresponding activities occurred in most other countries bordering the North Sea, and it soon became clear that not only were the problems common, but that it would require a common co-operative approach to solve them. As a

47

result, in 1902 was founded the International Council for the Exploration of the Sea (I.C.E.S.). This, the oldest of the many international bodies concerned with research or management of marine fisheries, is responsible for stimulating and co-ordinating most aspects of scientific research in the waters of the North-east Atlantic, but has since its beginnings given particular attention to the problems of overfishing and management. In this regard one of its most significant achievements has been in the compilation of comprehensive statistics of the fisheries of the area. These have been published annually (with some gaps in war-time) in the I.C.E.S. *Bulletin Statistique*. They give an unrivalled basis for the quantitative study of the fish stocks, and with the sometimes more detailed national statistics, which were often developed on the initiative of I.C.E.S., have provided the main basis of the activities of the various international working groups on the assessment of different stocks, which in the past fifteen years or so have in turn provided the scientific advice for management. (It may be noted that the Bureau of International Whaling Statistics, which provided most of the statistics for the quantitative studies of Antarctic whale stocks, was set up on the suggestion of I.C.E.S.)

While these statistics were to be the major element of scientific activity in later years, for the first couple of decades of I.C.E.S.' existence the statistical series were not long enough, nor were the techniques of analysis sufficiently developed, for useful analysis to be made. The main scientific attention was rather turned to learning the basic facts about the natural history of the commercial species. The period up to the outbreak of the first world war saw a remarkable accumulation of information about the fishes of the North Sea—their growth, as determined by the reading of scales or otoliths; their migrations, from tagging experiments; and their general distribution. Much of this original work is contained in extremely bulky volumes of reports, and has been summarized in later review studies on particular species, e.g. on cod (Graham, 1948) and plaice (Wimpenny, 1953).

During the pre-war period the first attempts were made at the positive improvement of the fish stocks through the hatching of eggs of cod and other species, and the transplanting of small plaice from the crowded grounds of the Baltic where growth is slow, to the faster growing areas of the North Sea. In the half century since then these activities have been in and out of fashion, but little real progress has been achieved, despite the attractions

48

of these ideas to those who like to talk about bringing fishing out of the primitive hunting stage into the age of agriculture. Partly this has been due to technical difficulties—it is not too difficult a matter to hatch out a million cod eggs, but not so easy to rear the young fish to a size at which they can be released in the sea with any reasonable chance of survival. Partly the difficulty is directly connected with the problems of management; it is hardly worth while the Danish Government or industry transplanting small plaice to the Dogger Bank, however fast they grow when they arrive, if most of them are going to be fished up by English or Dutch fishermen, rather than by Danes.

After the first war most of the scientific effort was concentrated mainly on the continuation of the basic survey and biological studies, but important steps were taken in developing techniques for the quantitative study of the population dynamics of fish stocks. While after the war-time increase in the fish stocks there was general agreement that fishing could, and had, reduced the stocks of demersal fish, it was less clear what could be done about it. Without some theoretical basis to determine the quantitative relation between the total amount of fishing, or the sizes of fish caught, and the total yield, it was difficult to persuade people that fishing at a moderate rate could produce more fish than heavy fishing. Important steps had in fact been made in developing a theoretical model by the Russian scientist F. I. Baranov, in a paper published at the end of the war (Baranov, 1918), but a more unfortunate time and place to publish original ideas would be hard to choose, and his theories gained little attention until after similar methods had been developed elsewhere.

Suitable methods were in fact developed toward the end of the inter-war period, notably by Michael Graham and E. S. Russel. *Table 5* below, adapted from Graham (1948), shows how the same catch in weight could be caught by moderate or heavy fishing. The example, taken to represent the North Sea cod situation, probably overestimates the fishing mortality and underestimates the natural mortality. On the other hand, no allowance was made for fish older than four years, which would be numerous for the moderate rate of exploitation.

Though the algebra of this particular example does not bear too close examination—the survival under heavy fishing seems high compared with the catches—the principle is clear and readily understood. Though adequate as a demonstration—and a mechanical analogue on the pin-ball principle was later constructed as an educational toy for visitors to the Lowestoft Laboratory (Richardson and Gulland, 1958), modifications were needed to provide an adequate tool for management. These were provided by the post-war studies of Beverton and Holt (1957), in which the rather clumsy and tedious year-by-year arithmetical calculations

Table 5.—RELATIVE CATCHES UNDER HEAVY AND LIGHT FISHING.
(*From* Graham, 1948.)

	HEAVY FISHING				MODERATE FISHING			
Age	1	2	3	4	1	2	3	4
Average weight	$\frac{1}{4}$	1	3	6	$\frac{1}{4}$	1	3	6
Stock (numbers)	20	8	3	1	20	14	10	7
Catch (numbers)	18	7	3	1	6	4	3	2
Catch (weight)	$4\frac{1}{2}$	7	9	6	$1\frac{1}{2}$	4	9	12
Total catch (weight)	$26\frac{1}{2}$				$26\frac{1}{2}$			

of *Table* 5 were replaced by algebraic computations covering the whole exploited lifespan, essentially as described in the next chapter. Methods were also set out to deal with possible second-order effects, such as changes in growth with changes in abundance.

The computations of Beverton and Holt were mainly based on the analysis of the inter-war fishery on plaice in the North Sea. The essence of their findings are given in *Fig.* 6, which is an isopleth diagram relating yield (given by the contour lines) simultaneously to the amount of fishing (along the *x*-axis) and to the age at first capture (on the *y*-axis). The mean position of the inter-war fishing is indicated by P. During this period the fishery changed little, and it was not easy to check the validity of this model. Since then there have been substantial changes in both the amount of fishing and in the sizes of fish being caught. It is very pleasing that the changes in catches following these changes have fitted the prediction very closely (Gulland, 1968). The trends in total catch, effort, and catch per unit effort are shown in *Fig.* 7. This shows that though there were high catches immediately after the war, they decreased rapidly and it seemed that the fishery was rapidly returning to its unhappy pre-war situation. However, the effort never increased to its pre-war level, so that there was much better year-to-year survival of the fish (*see Fig.* 8).

There were also important changes in the sizes of plaice that were caught. In the eastern North Sea these occurred around 1940, when the Danes adopted the Danish seine instead of the otter trawl as their main method of plaice fishing. They used a

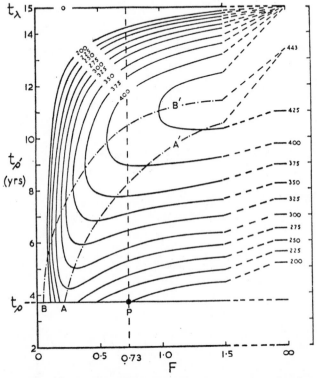

Fig. 6.—Yield isopleth diagram for North Sea plaice, showing yield per recruit as a function of fishing mortality, and size at first capture. (*From* Beverton and Holt, 1957.)

much larger mesh in the seine (*c.* 125 mm., instead of *c.* 70 mm. in the trawl) so that fewer very small fish were caught. In addition the Danish seine is a much gentler gear than the trawl, so that what small unmarketable fish that were caught arrived on the deck in good condition, and probably a fair number survived after being discarded. It may be noted that most unmarketable fish that are caught by commercial fishermen do not survive the experience; by the time the fishermen have dealt with their more urgent task of dealing with the marketable fish, and setting the

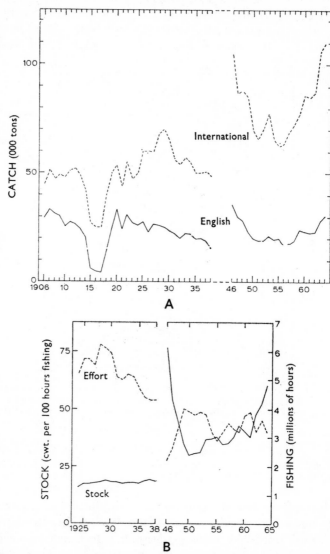

Fig. 7.—**A**, Annual landings of North Sea Plaice, 1906–64. **B**, Trends in corresponding fishing effort (broken line) and estimated stock abundance (catch per 100 hours fishing) by English trawlers. (*From* Gulland, 1968.)

gear for the next haul, and turn to shovelling the unwanted fish back into the sea, most are dead. Plaice, however, are extremely tough, and if not too damaged in the trawl can survive on the normally cold and damp deck of the average North Sea trawler

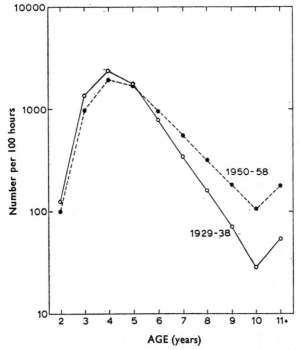

Fig. 8.—Numbers of plaice of successive ages caught in 100 hours fishing by English trawlers (logarithmic scale) to show better survival in post-war years. (*From* Gulland, 1968.)

for several hours. In this case, but in few others, a size limit has direct value.

In the case of the English fishery the change came later, around 1955. At that time the old steam trawlers were being replaced by new and more powerful motor trawlers, capable of working effectively in the deeper and more distant parts of the North Sea. In these areas the larger plaice had always been relatively more abundant—in fact the increase in average size with increasing depth has been dignified by the name of Heincke's Law (Heincke, 1913), but so long as the heavy fishing on the younger fish allowed few to survive, the total number of large fish on these deeper grounds was low. In 1955, though, the modern trawlers found an abundance of large fish, and the centre of English plaice fishing shifted to these grounds, leading to a sharp increase in the average size caught, and a decrease in the number of plaice under 30 cm.

As a result of these two changes, less fishing and a larger size at first capture, fishing has improved almost exactly as could be predicted from the theory. However, these changes were accidental, rather than the result of conscious management measures. It seems all too likely that following this improvement—and also the relatively poorer fishing outside the North Sea—fishing will be attracted back to the North Sea, fishermen will have to go after the small fish, because not enough large fish will have survived the attentions of other fishermen, and conditions will return to the pre-war state.

Mesh Regulation

While this clear demonstration of the effect of taking the right actions—even in this case accidentally—did not occur until recently, the scientists were using the theoretical models before the war to show what the benefits could be, and to urge appropriate action. Since the smallest size of plaice (and also haddock and cod) being caught was so much less than their potential size, the improvement in total catch from increasing the size at first capture was of the same order as the increase from reducing the amount of fishing. Control of the latter requires the unpleasant step of telling some or all the fishermen to stop fishing for all or some of the time, while in the North Sea trawl fisheries control of the size at first capture appeared to be readily achievable by suitable regulation of the mesh size in the trawl.

The first steps toward international management were therefore the setting of appropriate mesh regulations. Despite much discussion no firm agreement was reached before the war, but in 1946, in the same spirit of setting up a clean new world and avoiding the errors of the past which had seen the founding of the United Nations and many other more specialized international bodies, including the International Whaling Commission, there was signed in London the Overfishing Convention. Under this the countries of north-west Europe agreed to set maximum mesh sizes, and also to set minimum landing sizes for the main species of demersal fish (many such minimum sizes were already in effect under various national regulations). At the 1946 Conference it was also agreed that it would be desirable to reduce the total effort to 85 per cent of the 1936–38 level, but no action was taken on this. Even the action on mesh size did not actually take place until 1954.

The theory behind mesh regulation is simple. The bigger the mesh size in the trawl, the bigger the fish that can get through it. If, to obtain the best yield, fish should not be caught before they

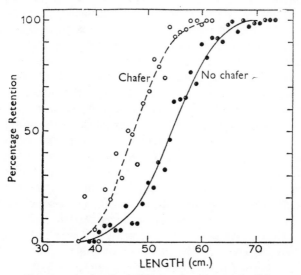

Fig. 9.—Percentage of cod of different lengths retained by a cod end with a 130-mm. mesh, showing the spread of selection, and the effect of an attachment to the top of the net. (*From* I.C.E.S., 1966.)

reach 30 cm., then the mesh size used should be such as to just allow fish of 30 cm. to escape through the net, but to retain any bigger fish. A minimum landing size of 30 cm. should also be set to eliminate any incentive to use a smaller mesh size. It was with such rather simple ideas in mind that the 1946 Convention came into being, and the next couple of decades in the North Atlantic could well be termed the age of mesh regulation.

The simple theory of mesh regulation faced a number of practical difficulties which obstructed its quick and easy introduction. The chief of these were that the optimum mesh size was different for each species, that selection was not sharp, so that a net which would let most of the desired fish escape would also let many much larger fish escape, and that the precise selectivity of the net, i.e. the sizes of fish released, depends on the type of twine and the type of net, the presence or absence of attachments (chafing gear) to the net as well as on the actual geometrical dimensions of the mesh (*see Fig.* 9). Difficulties also arose over the enforcement of regulations after they were adopted.

The first of these difficulties, the difference in optimum mesh for different species, was recognized in the 1946 Convention. This distinguished two groups of species. The first group was the demersal species whose conservation and management were the purpose of the mesh regulation. Any temptation by fishermen to circumvent the mesh regulation was supposed to be reduced by the imposition of minimum sizes of the fish that could be landed. For each species these sizes were listed in Annex II of the Convention. The other group was the small fish that required a smaller mesh size for their effective capture than that used in the normal trawl fishery. These were listed in Article 6 of the Convention, and these so-called Article 6 species included pelagic fish such as herring and mackerel, as well as shrimps and prawns.

So far as it went this provided a solution to some parts of the problem. Herring trawling and shrimp fishing are quite separate from normal trawling for bottom fish, such as plaice or cod—conveniently if not entirely scientifically classed as 'white fish' in the British Isles, and looked after by a White Fish Authority which is quite separate from the Herring Industry Board. Though trawls may be used in each case the details of the design and rigging are quite different, and there is no real practical difficulty, or problem of enforcement, involved in setting different legal mesh sizes in the different fisheries.

One problem did arise, and has been discussed in detail by a special Committee set up by the Permanent Commission, which is the question of the so-called by-catch (I.C.E.S., 1960). Though fishermen engaged in an Article 6 fishery, e.g. herring trawling, do not deliberately fish for other species, it is inevitable that some other fish will occasionally get into the net. Since the herring trawl has a small mesh, small haddock or cod very much less than the optimum size, or the size retained by the legal white fish trawl, will be retained. If the number of these small fish in the by-catch is large, then the Article 6 fishery could have a significant effect on the other fisheries which might have later caught these fish after they had grown. The extent of this effect varies quite widely, as regards both the species in the by-catch, and the type of small-meshed fishery. The biggest effects seem to have been that of the herring trawl fishery on the later fishery for whiting, when the catches of the latter may be reduced by some 15 per cent by the operations of the herring trawlers (I.C.E.S., 1960). Flatfish (sole and plaice) are rarely caught in herring trawls, but quantitities of of small plaice are caught in shrimp trawls. No estimate of their effect was made, though the Committee thought that it might be considerable. However, since 1960 modifications have been devised to the shrimp trawl which hopefully will reduce this by-catch. Essentially this is a large-meshed filter in the bottom of the trawl through which the fish, which tend to escape downward, will pass, while retaining the shrimp which try to escape upward. Altogether it was found that while the use of small meshes by the Article 6 fishermen did cause damage to the other fishermen, this damage was always considerably less than the value of the Article 6 fisheries, which could not be carried out with larger meshes. Therefore, considering the management of the fisheries in the North Sea as a whole, the use of the small mesh was justified, disappointing as this no doubt was to the haddock or plaice fishermen.

Another intractable problem was that of the different sizes of individual fish and of optimum mesh size for different species of normal bottom fish, or 'white fish'. The two problem species in the North Sea were the whiting and the sole. The research on which the main conclusions on mesh regulations had been based were the cod, plaice, and haddock. The cod is large, and the plaice, though smaller, is an awkward shape to slip through the meshes, and for both the optimum mesh size is large—well over 100 mm.—the precise value depending on the stock and the current intensity of fishing on the stock. The haddock is rather smaller than cod, but in the North Sea would still benefit from a mesh size considerably larger than that current in the North Sea around 1946 which was probably about 60 mm., though varying from fleet to fleet. On the basis of analysis of these three species at the time of signing of the 1946 Convention it was expected that the introduction of an 80 mm. mesh for the North Sea trawl fisheries would be achieved, with further increases later.

Several other of the species taken in these fisheries would also benefit from a large mesh size, but catches of sole and whiting would be seriously affected by a mesh as large as 80 mm. Both are relatively small, and while the sole is a flatfish like the plaice, it is long and narrow with a great ability to wriggle through the meshes. In terms of the North Sea fisheries as a whole some loss of these fish by using a larger mesh would be more than made up by the larger gains in catches of cod, haddock, and plaice. However, there are some fishermen who catch much more than the average share of sole and whiting (mainly Dutch and Scottish respectively), and who would not be at all happy to see their catches reduced for the benefit of English or German fishermen. For them the optimum mesh size would be not much more than about 70–75 mm., and even this would mean quite a delicate balance between the immediate loss of small to medium size fish through the meshes and the long-term benefit of increased catches of medium to large fish.

The unwillingness of certain fishermen to accept the proposed general increase of mesh size to 80 mm. for all the North Sea demersal fisheries was reinforced by differences in selectivity between types of net. The original calculations of the right mesh size to use, insofar as these had been formal calculations, rather than an unquantified, though quite correct feeling that the present mesh size was too small, had been based largely on the English trawl fishery. These ships use a fairly heavy net, made in those days usually of double manila twine, often heavily tarred to preserve it. This twine was not at all flexible, so the meshes were not easy for the fish to wriggle through.

At the other extreme were some of the seine nets used by Scottish fishermen, which were made of light flexible material, usually thin cotton twine. For mesh of given geometrical dimensions, much larger fish could get through a cotton seine net than through a heavy manila trawl. The seine fishermen would therefore release more fish, but share any later benefit from them with the trawl fishermen. Unfortunately, this acted in the same way as the differential between largely the same groups of fishermen as regards differences in species, and made it even more difficult for some, such as the Scottish fishermen, to accept the original proposal for a uniform 80 mm. The solution to this problem was to allow different mesh sizes for different types of net, with the hope that with appropriate differentials the actual sizes of fish released by each net would be the same. This was never achieved in practice. About the time that the existence of differences between materials became known the simple situation in which only two or three natural fibres were used (manila, sisal, and cotton), was radically altered by the introduction of an ever-increasing range of synthetics of different basic chemistry, usually with several different trade names, each of which could be made up in a variety of ways.

This led to a great number of experiments being carried out to determine the selectivity for each new type of twine (I.C.E.S., 1964), a series which slowly came to an end as it became obvious that, given the variety of types of net possible, and the great difficulty of determining with great precision exactly what sizes of fish escaped through a net, it would never be possible to ensure complete equivalence in relation between all nets used (Gulland, 1964a). The main effect of attempting this had been that too much attention of scientists and administrators was deflected from other matters to argue over small details of difference in selectivity.

These arguments were made particularly irrelevant by the absence of any general enforcement of the minimum mesh size regulation to the degree of precision implied by the discussions over selectivity differentials. The measurement of the size of mesh in a net is not an exact matter. Individual meshes in the same net vary, and can be stretched by act of measurement. Regulations have been made in terms of allowing a gauge of a certain width to pass 'easily' through the meshes. Depending on the force to thrust the gauge into the mesh, and the interpretation of 'easily', a difference of up to 15 per cent can be obtained in the size of the smallest mesh that could be passed as legal.

These problems, which with strict enforcement of the regulations could result in an average mesh size in use quite different from the legal minimum, were less important than the effects of an absence of good enforcement. Initially, the enforcement of the recommendations was wholly a national matter, based on appropriate national legislation. Soon after the international agreement on mesh regulation came into force it became clear that enforcement was not being applied with equal force in all countries. Not only did this mean that the full beneficial effects on the stocks were not being produced, and such benefits as did occur were being distributed unequally, but also, once the laxness of enforcement in one country became apparent, proper enforcement elsewhere became more difficult. Fishing boats are often putting into foreign ports, for urgent repairs, or to shelter from bad weather, and the local fishermen are naturally quick to notice whether or not the foreigner's gear conforms with the regulations. If it does not, then the locals are much less willing to follow the regulations themselves. This can threaten the whole structure of the management since conformity of the fishermen to the regulations depends more on persuading them that the rules are for their benefit than on direct police-type enforcement.

Much attention has therefore been paid to devising some pattern of international control, or inspection, so that fishermen of each country can be satisfied that the others are abiding by the rules. With such diverse, and mutually distrustful countries as, for example, Spain and U.S.S.R. being concerned, agreement on any scheme which would involve the right to some degree of inter-ference by, say, Spanish authorities with Russian trawlers fishing on the high seas, has been difficult. Nevertheless, a scheme has been introduced, which while not going as far as giving any right of enforcement, in the sense of instituting prosecutions, over foreign vessels on the high seas, does allow duly authorized officers on board specified vessels flying the proper pennant, to stop any fishing vessel to inspect it. If there is evidence that the rules are being broken, e.g. that the mesh size is too small, then the facts are reported to the government of the country concerned for appropriate action (*see* Reports of the North East Atlantic Fisheries Commission, and of the International Commission for the North-west Atlantic Fisheries). While the arrangements are not perfect—for instance some countries at present only allow inspectors to look at the nets on deck and do not allow them to go below deck, and in return inspectors of these countries are limited to above-deck inspection—there is enough authority to build up a proper international confidence that the rules are being generally obeyed.

At the same time as the compliance with the mesh regulations was being improved, their scope was being widened. On the western side of the North Atlantic mesh regulations were at first applied only to the haddock fishery on Georges Bank. As fishing elsewhere built up it soon seemed probable that the bottom fisheries in other parts of the North-west Atlantic would benefit from such regulation, provided that the size of mesh was suitably chosen, and that the mesh sizes in several parts of the North-east Atlantic could also with advantage be increased. As a result the scientists became deeply involved in calculating for each of the major demersal stocks, the immediate and long-term effects of changes in mesh sizes (Gulland, 1961, 1964b). The largest study was made by a working group set up by I.C.N.A.F., which worked between 1959 and 1961 carrying out a review on the available data for the whole I.C.N.A.F. area (Beverton and Hodder, 1962). Many other groups were set up to study individual stocks, and their reports can be found in the general reports of the I.C.E.S. Liaison Committee to N.E.A.F.C., or of the Research and Statistics Committee of I.C.N.A.F.

One of the most significant by-products of these groups was that the scientists concerned became used to working closely together. Given the proper tradition that science knows no political boundaries this was perhaps not too difficult. In many ways it was more difficult to overcome another strong, if less well-publicized, scientific tradition of holding on to original data until they can be incorporated into appropriate personal publications. The working groups found it necessary, in the face of usually very sparse information, to make sure that all available data were put together, perhaps using data on catch per unit effort from the English fishery, measurements of fish length from the Russian fishery, and Norwegian observations on the ages of fish. One way or another it was usually possible to produce an analysis and a report advising the relevant Commission on the most likely effect of using various mesh sizes, which could be accepted by the Commission as being the best scientific advice. Thus arguments on scientific questions were not raised in the Commission itself. These traditions of close scientific collaboration, and of keeping scientific arguments outside the Commission, became established during this period of study of the effects of mesh changes, which generally did not raise difficult questions of national interest. However, they seem to have survived into a later period, in which possible limitation of the amount of fishing can cause grave national problems.

Following these scientific studies, though usually with a certain amount of delay while governments and industries argued about the necessity or urgency of acting on the scientific evidence, a minimum mesh size was introduced, or the current one increased, in most of the demersal fisheries of the North Atlantic. By about 1965 action in this direction had gone as far as was practicable. Where the regulation mesh size was still below the optimum for some or most of the stocks in any area, further increase was made difficult by the existence of stocks of smaller species in the area. The scientists were also pointing out strongly that mesh regulation could solve only some of the problems. Thus the Commissions, and their member countries, turned, somewhat reluctantly, from their reasonably successful introduction of control of the sizes of fish caught, to tackling the more substantial problems of controlling the total amount of fishing.

Control of the Amount of Fishing

The desirability of limiting the amount of fishing, and hence, in principle, the total costs of fishing, has been known for a long time. Almost as soon as scientists could calculate the benefits of the use of an increased mesh size, they were also pointing out the limitations of such measures as the sole method of management. Not only does mesh limitation fail to control the input (effort, costs) into the fishery, but to the extent that it is successful it will tend to encourage more effort. The more the stock, and the catches per unit effort, are increased by the use of a larger mesh, the more attractive will fishing become. This will encourage more vessels to enter the fishery, until the increased effort depresses the catch per unit effort back to its original level.

While these theoretical calculations are obvious, it is less obvious what can be done about the situation. The problem was recognized at the time of preparation of the 1946 Overfishing Convention which set as its target in the North Sea the use of an 80 mm. mesh (as already noted), and also the limitation of the total amount of fishing to 85 per cent of the pre-war value. This immediately met two difficulties—first there was the problem of determining what consituted 85 per cent of the pre-war level of fishing effort, in a fishery with a variety of different sizes and types of ships, and involving a number of different species of fish; second, some countries, which were developing their fisheries, especially on a number of species, such as sand-eels, which were not known to be heavily exploited, could not agree to such a simplified measure, which could prevent the full utilization of such underexploited stocks.

The Permanent Commission, which carried out the objectives agreed on by the 1946 Convention, therefore did not concern itself with the question of controlling the amount of fishing. As it became clearer that mesh regulation was not enough, action was taken to make other regulations possible. A new convention was therefore drawn up by a conference held in London in January, 1959, which included considerations on regulation of the amount of total catch, or the amount of fishing effort. However, these latter measures were placed in a special paragraph, and could not be immediately considered by the new North East Atlantic Fisheries Commission until transferred by a two-thirds majority to the list of measures which could be recommended. Apart from the reasons above, a significant consideration for several countries in placing these important measures in a class by themselves was that of control and enforcement. While uneven enforcement of mesh regulation is very undesirable, and places those with the strictest enforcement at a disadvantage, this disadvantage is very small compared with that occurring if control of total catch or effort is not properly complied with.

On the eastern side of the Atlantic any concrete move to control the amount of fishing within the international commission is impossible until the necessary formal step to activate the relevant provision of the Convention has been made, which at present (February, 1972) has not been done though this is expected to come into operation in 1973*. On the western side there are not the same formal obstructions to introducing control of the amount of fishing. The relevant Commission (I.C.N.A.F.) was however for some time impeded at least as seriously by the way in which its general objectives were phrased, which were to obtain 'the maximum sustained catch' as opposed to N.E.A.F.C.'s objectives of 'conservation . . . and rational utilization'. This made it more difficult   ✗ ✗
for I.C.N.A.F. to take into account economic factors. This did not prevent I.C.N.A.F. seeking advice on economic factors. Following a report in 1965 from the Chairmen of its Research and Statistics Committee, and its Assessment Subcommittee (Templeman and Gulland, 1965), which reviewed the possible conservation actions that I.C.N.A.F. could take, including the large potential economic benefit from control of input, I.C.N.A.F. set up, with the co-operation of F.A.O., a joint group of biologists and economists to examine the subject in more detail. This group met twice in 1967 and its report (I.C.N.A.F., 1968) pointed out both the theoretical advantages from controlling the amount of fishing on a heavily fished stock, and the fact that most of the cod and haddock stocks in the I.C.N.A.F. area were already heavily exploited, and the effort was continuing to increase.

---

*This had not come into force by June, 1973, because one country—Iceland—had not yet ratified the agreement.

The main part of this steady increase, so far as the cod and haddock stocks were concerned, had been the large cod stocks from the Grand Banks of Newfoundland northward to West Greenland. These large stocks have attracted European fleets for four centuries, and were now attracting the fleets of new large freezer trawlers, as well as newly-built fleets of medium sized locally-based trawlers supplying fish to the freezing factories in Newfoundland and Nova Scotia.

It is therefore somewhat ironic that the first measures taken by I.C.N.A.F. to control the total amount of fishing was in the most southerly part of the area, for the haddock on Georges Bank, on which on the whole the amount of fishing was not tending to increase. There had, however, been a series of events which made some emergency action desirable and acceptable. This stock of haddock had been heavily fished for a long time, almost entirely by the local U.S. fleet, and had benefited by the first regulatory measure introduced by I.C.N.A.F.—the use of a larger ($4\frac{1}{2}$ in.) mesh size in this fishery. As in most haddock stocks fluctuations in year-class strength have always occurred in the Georges Bank stocks, but until recently these were not violent and annual catches varied between 40,000 and 60,000 tons. In 1962, and again in 1963, an extremely good year-class was produced. This entered the fishery just as a large Russian fleet, which had developed a big fishery for silver hake in the area, was looking for alternative supplies. In barely a year—in the second half of 1965 and the beginning of 1966—the Russians caught around 150,000 tons, and the total catch reached 155,000 tons in 1965 and 127,000 tons in 1966. By the end of 1966 the two year-classes of 1962 and 1963, originally so strong, had been reduced to no more than about average strength. This would not have been serious except that the following year-classes, certainly up till that of 1970, if not later, were all poor or extremely poor. As a result the stock abundance, which had been somewhat above average in 1966, steadily declined, with no prospects of any recovery until a good new year-class should occur.

While the reason for the run of poor year-classes since 1963 is not known—and probably no single reason exists—there is a suspicious and worrying correlation between the recent poor year-classes from 1968 onward and the low parent abundance. If this correlation is indeed cause and effect, the only hope of getting good recruitment would be to maintain the adult stock at as high a level as possible, i.e. to reduce catches as much as possible. I.C.N.A.F. at its 1969 meeting therefore agreed to introduce a limit to the total catch of haddock on Georges Bank, as well as a total ban on trawling on the main spawning areas during the spawning season. This latter regulation, in principle unnecessary, was introduced partly as an extra protection at a time when the remaining stock was concentrated in a small area, and therefore particularly vulnerable, and partly to spread catches more evenly through the year.

By 1969 the haddock stocks were so low that no long-range fishery for haddock existed, and virtually all the haddock were taken by the local U.S. fleet, with a little by Canadian ships. There was therefore little problem of national allocation, or of the difficulties or unrestricted competition for an unallocated quota. Nevertheless, the first step had been taken toward control of the amount of fishing in the North-west Atlantic. This was followed in 1972 by the much more significant and important actions of setting quotas for many of the most important stocks of cod, herring, and other species, and also allocating shares in each quota to individual member countries of I.C.N.A.F. Meanwhile on the eastern side, though the constitutional obstructions had not been completely cleared, close consideration had been given to control of the amount of fishing, especially on the Arcto-Norwegian cod stock. This stock had by 1971 reached a state similar to that of the Georges Bank stock; though on a much larger scale—catches in peak years had exceeded one million tons, making this stock one of the most valuable single stocks in the world. Heavy fishing, and a run of poor year-classes, the latter correlated with, but not necessarily caused by, low parent stocks, had brought the stock to a low level with no immediate prospect for recovery.

The countries mainly concerned—Norway, U.K., and U.S.S.R. —had therefore consulted together to determine how restrictions could be applied to rebuild the stock. Though agreement was close, it was not quite reached. Partly this was the difficulty of agreeing on how the total catch should be allocated—this was particularly difficult because the English and Russians were mainly fishing young fish, and the Norwegians adult fish, on the average 4 years older, so that one country might be harvesting good year-classes, and another weak ones—and partly the feeling that any agreement would be largely self-defeating unless part of a larger system of control for the North Atlantic cod fisheries as a whole.

Most of the cod fishing fleets, especially the freezer-trawlers, are highly mobile, and can fish, say, off northern Russia on one trip, and off Newfoundland on the next trip six weeks later. If one ground is closed or restricted, then the effort that would have been expended there would go elsewhere. Since most if not all the cod stocks are fully exploited, any of the benefit of reduced fishing say on the Arcto-Norwegian stock would be balanced by the effects of increased fishing at Labrador or elsewhere. This was clearly pointed out by the I.C.N.A.F. bio-economics group (I.C.N.A.F., 1968), and more recently recognized by the setting up, in 1971, of a joint I.C.N.A.F.-I.C.E.S. working group to examine the state of the stocks of the Atlantic cod as a whole.

In summary, therefore, the history of the North Atlantic bottom fishing has been of two phases—expansion and management. The beginnings of the expansion phase are lost in pre-history; later came the development of the salt cod fishery, now several hundred years old, and since the coming of the steam trawler expansion was continuous and fairly steady for a hundred years. This phase is now reaching its end.

The management phase began with biological studies which showed the need for and benefits from proper management. It has progressed to the setting up of the necessary international machinery for implementing necessary action, as well as for providing the needed scientific advice before taking action, and some measure of verification, on an international basis, that the recommended action has indeed been taken by all participants. The last, and most difficult step, of actually taking substantive action, has only been started. The less painful, but less beneficial measures of controlling mesh size (and also sizes of fish landed) have been successfully introduced. The actions of I.C.N.A.F. in 1972 give hope that the more difficult measures to control the amount of fishing can be brought into operation with equal success, and hopefully more rapidly.

REFERENCES

ALWARD, G. L. (1932), *The Sea Fisheries of Great Britain and Ireland.* Grimsby: Albert Gait.

ATKINSON, G. T. (1908), 'Notes on a fishing voyage to the Barents Sea in August, 1907', *J. Mar. Biol. Ass. U.K.*, **8,** 71–98.

BARANOV, F. I. (1918), 'On the question of the biological basis of fisheries', *Nauchnyi Issledoratelskii ikhtiologecheskii Institut. Isvestia*, **1** (1), 81–128.

BEVERTON, R. J. H., and HODDER, V. M. (1962), 'Report of the working group of scientists on fishery assessment in relation to regulation problems', *Ann. Proc. int. Commiss. N.W. Atlant. Fish.*, **11** suppl., 81.

BEVERTON, R. J. H., and HOLT, S. J. (1957), 'On the dynamics of exploited fish populations', *Fish. Invest., Lond.*, ser. 2, **19,** 533.

GRAHAM, H. W. (1954), 'Conserving New England haddock', *Trans. 19th N. Amer. Wildlife Conf.*, 397–402.

GRAHAM, M. (1948), *Rational Fishing of the Cod of the North Sea*, 111. London: Edward Arnold.

GULLAND, J. A. (1961), 'The estimation of the effect on catches of changes in gear selectivity', *J. Cons. int. Explor. Mer*, **26**(2), 204–14.

GULLAND, J. A. (1964a), 'Variations in selection factor and mesh differentials', *J. Cons. int. Explor. Mer*, **29**(2), 158–65.

GULLAND, J. A. (1964b), 'A note on the interim effects on catches of changes in gear selectivity', *J. Cons. int. Explor. Mer*, **29**(1), 61–4.

GULLAND, J. A. (1968), 'Recent changes in the North Sea plaice fishery', *J. Cons. int. Explor. Mer*, **31**(3), 305–22.

GULLAND, J. A. (1972), *The Fish Resources of the Ocean* (ed.). London: Fishing News (Books) Ltd.

HEINCKE, F. (1913), 'Investigations on the plaice. General Report 1. The plaice fishery and protective regulations', *Rapp. Proc. Verb. Cons. int. Explor. Mer*, 17.

INNIS, H. A. (1954), *The Cod Fisheries*, 522. University of Toronto Press.

INTERNATIONAL COMMISSION FOR N.W. ATLANTIC FISHERIES (1968), 'Report of the Working Group on joint biological and economic assessment of conservation actions', *Ann. Proc. int. Commiss. N.W. Atlant. Fish.*, **17,** 48–84.

INTERNATIONAL COUNCIL FOR THE EXPLOITATION OF THE SEA (1960), 'Committee on mesh difficulties. Report of the Scientific sub-committee', *Rapp. Proc. Verb. Cons. int. Explor. Mer*, **151,** 39.

INTERNATIONAL COUNCIL FOR THE EXPLOITATION OF THE SEA (1964), 'Report of the mesh selection working group', *Co-op. Res. Rep. int. Coun. Explor. Sea*, **2,** 156.

INTERNATIONAL COUNCIL FOR THE EXPLORATION OF THE SEA (1954), 'Symposium on cod', *Rapp. Proc. Verb. Cons. int. Explor. Mer*, 136.

MORISON, S. E. (1971), *The European Discovery of America. The Northern Voyages.* New York: Oxford University Press.

RICHARDSON, I. D., and GULLAND, J. A. (1958), 'Description of a model used to demonstrate dynamics of exploited fish stocks', *J. Cons. int. Explor. Mer*, **24**(1), 55–9.

TEMPLEMAN, W. F., and GULLAND, J. A. (1965), 'Review of possible conservation actions for the I.C.N.A.F. area', *Ann. Proc. int. Commiss. N.W. Atlant. Fish.*, 15.

WIMPENNY, R. S. (1953), *The Plaice* (Buckland Lectures for 1949). London: Edward Arnold.

Chapter

4

THE BIOLOGICAL BASIS OF MANAGEMENT

ALL management of fisheries depends on biological information. Unless there is good information on the likely consequences of alternative management actions, no rational decision can be taken. This does not mean that the biologist is required to predict the results of, say, a 10 per cent reduction in fishing effort with absolute certainty, but the degree of uncertainty should be commensurate with the other uncertainties involved in making decisions concerned with the management of fishery enterprises, e.g. doubts about the future prices of fish products, the cost of new vessels, etc.

In making his predictions, the fishery scientist must use some model of the fish population. These models consist of mathematical expressions, sometimes quite simple, and in other cases more complex, which represent the events that occur in the fish stock in the sea. In the model the results can be studied of possible management actions, such as controls on the amount of fishing or of the sizes of fish caught. If the model is a useful one to the manager a whole range of possible actions can be analysed, and the results predicted by the model will correspond reasonably closely to what would actually happen in practice. Given the complexities of any natural system such as stock of fish in the ocean, and the great number of things that might affect it other than fishing, no model can give an absolutely accurate prediction of the course of events. The chief requirement of a model in the present context is that it should enable the right choice to be made between alternative management actions.

The models used by fisheries can be conveniently grouped into two; those that treat the fish population as a whole, considering the changes in total biomass, without reference to its structure (age composition, etc.), and those that consider the population as

68

the sum of its individuals, and are concerned with the growth and mortality rates of the individuals. The former type of model is particularly associated with the work of Schaefer (1954, 1957), though outlined earlier in the sigmoid curve model of Graham (1939). The second, a dynamic pool model, is particularly associated with the work of Ricker (1948, 1958) and Beverton and Holt (1957), though again the origins are much earlier, in works such as those of Baranov (1918). A general review of the methods of applying these models to the assessment of exploited fish stocks is given by Gulland (1969).

The Logistic Model and Its Developments

The logistic model used by Schaefer, and the similar models treating the population as a single unit, have great advantages of simplicity. They demand only the simplest types of data for their application and their theoretical basis may be easily understood. They are based on the simple, general models of population growth. These stated that the biomass (B) of a population will tend to increase until the population has reached the limit of the carrying capacity of the environment. The rate of increase will be determined solely by the current abundance, or biomass, of the population, that is in mathematical terms:

$$\frac{dB}{dt} = f(B)$$

Limits to the form of $f(B)$ are set by the fact that it will be zero when the population is zero. It will also tend to zero at the equilibrium level, B_0, at which the population will tend to stabilize in the absence of exploitation. Once at this level the population will not change except for fluctuations of greater or smaller amplitude due to year-to-year changes in environmental conditions. That is, considering average conditions, we can write:

$$f(O) = 0$$
$$f(B_0) = 0$$

For populations between zero and B_0, the rate of increase will be positive. As the population increases from zero the rate of increase will rise to a maximum at some intermediate value and then decrease (cf. *Fig.* 3). At this stage no assumptions are made about the precise form of the curve.

The same idea can be thought of in terms of the history of expansion of a small population of animals when introduced into a new environment. At first, when its absolute size is small, it will increase slowly, but then, as the population begins to expand the rate of increase in numbers per unit time will accelerate. After a time the population will begin to reach the carrying capacity of the environment (food supply, etc.), and the rate of increase will slow down. The population will tend asymptotically towards its maximum equilibrium level. This tendency is shown in *Fig.* 10A, the sigmoid curve of Graham (1939). The slope of this curve is equal to the value of the net rate of natural increase. If this slope is plotted against the size of the population (*Fig.* 10B), this gives the same curve as in *Fig.* 3.

If during any year man removes an amount equal to the natural annual increase, then the population abundance will remain unaltered. This removal could, therefore, be repeated each year indefinitely, and may be termed the 'sustainable yield', or 'equilibrium catch'. In particular, if the population were maintained at the level corresponding to the maximum in the curve of *Fig.* 3, then the equilibrium catch will be at its greatest, i.e., the maximum sustainable yield will be taken. Though the curves of *Figs.* 3 and 10 and the model on which they are based are highly simplified descriptions of the changes in a fish stock under exploitation, they do illustrate most of the biological features important to fishery management. The first is that it is impossible to exploit a fish stock without causing some change. This may seem obvious, but with the present-day concern with the natural environment, and the desire to minimize ecological disturbance, there may be a feeling that a well-managed fishery should cause no changes, which is impossible. Another form of the same thought is the belief, most often expressed by the established fishermen, that a falling abundance, as evidenced by a falling catch rate, in itself denotes too heavy fishing. This is not so, since the population may be still on the right hand part of the curve, in which worthwhile increases in yield would still be obtained by fishing harder and reducing to some extent the stock.

The second important point is almost the converse of this. That is, provided the catches are not too great, the decline in abundance is not continual. After a time the population will reach a new equilibrium, at which the same catches can be maintained indefinitely year after year. Finally, if the stock is allowed to be depleted too far, though still without driving it to extinction, its productivity and the catches that can be taken will be reduced.

The models discussed here, of both types, are basically concerned with determining the productivity, or sustainable yield, obtainable from different conditions of the fish population, and the pattern of fishing required to maintain the population in its optimum condition.

In this general statement no assumption is made about the forms of $f(B)$, provided that it satisfies the condition that $f(O) = o = f(B_0)$.

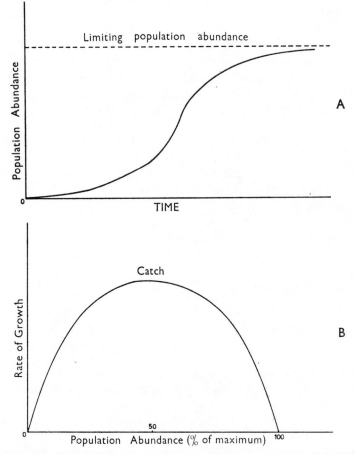

Fig. 10.—The sigmoid curve of the growth of a population in a limited environment (**A**), and the corresponding relation between rate of growth and population abundance (**B**).

The simplest mathematical expression that does this and thus provides a quantitative prediction of the sustainable yield from different levels of stock abundance is,

$$f(B) = aB(B_0 - B), \text{ where a is a constant.}$$

The same expression can also be derived in other ways. For instance, the rate of natural increase might be expected for small populations to be proportional to the size of the population, i.e., $f(B) \propto B$, and that close to the limiting size the rate of increase is proportional to the difference between the limiting population and the current size, i.e., $f(B) \propto (B_0 - B)$; combining, these give again:

$$f(B) = aB(B - B_0)$$

In practical fishery situations another derivation can be obtained empirically from analysis of catch per unit effort data. The biomass of a population can rarely be measured directly, and in most fisheries the best index of abundance is the catch per unit effort, i.e., the catch taken by a standard unit of gear in unit time. As will be shown, the relation between net natural rate of increase and biomass can be determined from the relation between sustainable yield and catch per unit effort. If the population is in equilibrium, so that the catch taken is the sustainable yield, the latter expression contains only two distinct variables—the catch and the effort. It can, therefore, be rearranged in terms of a relation between effort and catch per unit effort. Clearly catch per unit effort (an index of biomass) decreases as the fishing effort increases. The simplest mathematical expression to describe this is the linear relation:

$$C/f = a - bf$$

or, rearranging terms,

$$f = -1/b \, (C/f - a),$$

and multiplying both sides by C/f:

$$C = -1/b \; C/f \, (C/f - a)$$

and, since the catch per unit will be approximately proportional to the biomass, we can write $C/f = qB$, where q is a constant and hence,

$$C = \frac{q^2}{b} B(B_0 - B), \text{ writing } B_0 = \frac{a}{q}.$$

These different derivations, however, prove no more about the logistic than that it is to bio-mathematicians a very common and convenient form. There is no proof that the fish stocks follow such simple laws. The last derivation shows most clearly how good the logistic is—it is as good as, and no better than, the simple linear approximation to the relation between two variables.

FITTING TO DATA

The last derivation is also in most situations the most convenient form to fitting the logistic to actual fishery data. In the simplest form this is merely a matter of plotting catch per unit effort against total effort and fitting a straight line.

There are a number of objections to this procedure. The first is purely statistical. If catch and effort are quite unconnected random variables, there will still be some correlation between catch per unit effort (c.p.u.e.) and effort simply from the way c.p.u.e. is calculated—a high effort will naturally result in a low catch per unit effort. Unless the true effort is very difficult to estimate, so that the main cause of variations in the observed catch per unit effort are due to random variations in the relation of recorded effort to true effort, rather than to actual variations in abundance, the degree of spurious correlation will be very small.

A more serious objection is that the catch, effort, and catch per unit effort in any particular year are not representative of an equilibrium situation. Thus the cod being fished in the North Sea in 1971 include fish born between 1964 and 1969. The initial numbers of fish of, say, the 1967 year-class when they entered the fishery in 1969 will have been determined, *inter alia*, by the abundance of adult cod in 1967 (and hence on the amount of fishing in 1967 and previous years). The number of survivors in 1971 depends on the amount of fishing since 1969. Their size will depend on their growth throughout their life, which will be related to the food supply, and hence to the abundance of cod then and over some previous period.

Clearly all these factors cannot be analysed without losing the essential simplicity of the approach. Usually variations in growth (and in natural mortality) are not large, and in most stocks fluctuations in year-class strength are only weakly correlated with parent abundance. The main influence of fishing is, therefore, the reduction in numbers of each year-class during the time they have been exposed to the fishing, which may range from a few days or months in the case of the youngest fish, up to perhaps five years for the oldest North Sea cod, or even more for longer-lived fish. The overall abundance of the stock can still not be related to the fishing effort during a single period of time, but a reasonable compromise is to relate the abundance at one instant of time to the mean fishing effort over a period up to that time, of duration equal to the average life-span of an individual fish in the fishery (Gulland, 1961). The approximation will be particularly close if the fishing effort, although not constant, has at least been subject to a fairly constant trend over a period. For instance, if the effort has been increasing, the most recent levels, which affect the youngest fish, will be higher than the average over the mean life-span, so that the youngest fish will be less abundant than if the average effort had been maintained. Conversely the oldest fish will have, during their lives, been subject to a mean level of fishing effort less than the recent average, and so will be more abundant. The overall abundance may, therefore, be quite close to that which would occur if the average effort in the past few years had been maintained long enough for the stock abundance to have reached equilibrium.

Plotting catch per unit effort against the mean effort will, therefore, give a relation approximately equal to the equilibrium relation between c.p.u.e. and effort. It is then a very simple matter of multiplication to deduce the equilibrium relation between catch and fishing effort (*Fig.* 11).

FISHING EFFORT

Correct measurement of fishing effort is clearly vital to the successful application of this method of analysis and before discussing in more detail the application of the population models, the methods of estimation of fishing effort need to be reviewed. Since the effort is considered as proportional to the parameter of real biological concern, the fishing mortality (and the c.p.u.e. proportional to the abundance), the absolute value is of no particular concern. The critical question is whether the relation between effort and mortality (or between c.p.u.e. and abundance) changes from year to year, especially if these changes show a consistant trend over a period, or are correlated with changes in stock abundance or the amount of fishing. Seasonal changes are likely to occur in relation to the migration, distribution, and behaviour of the fish, c.p.u.e. (and the mortality caused by a nominal unit effort) being highest when the fish are concentrated or otherwise particularly vulnerable to the gear. While these seasonal changes are often of vital practical importance to the fishermen—some fisheries are effectively restricted to the season

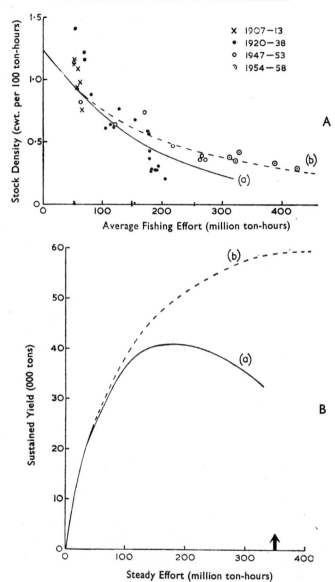

Fig. 11.—Observed relation between catch of haddock per unit fishing effort by English trawlers at Iceland, and the total amount of fishing (A), and corresponding relation between effort and total catch (B). Broken curve shows possible effect of recent changes in fishing practice. The arrow denotes the level of fishing effort in 1960. (*From* Gulland, 1961.)

of high availability—they are of less significance to the present study, which is concerned essentially with annual changes.

In a single, fairly homogeneous fleet, fishing effort is usually measured as the product of two terms, summed over all the units of the fleet—the fishing power of the individual unit, and the time spent fishing (Beverton and Holt, 1957; Gulland, 1956). At the simplest the fishing power of all boats might be taken as equal, and the fishing time equal to a year's operation. Then the fishing effort is merely equal to the number of vessels, and the c.p.u.e. is the catch per boat per year. Such a measure will be perfectly satisfactory as long as there are no changes in the average efficiency —fishing power—of the fleet (differences between vessels within the fleet are not in themselves of immediate significance if the composition of the fleet does not change), or in the effective amount of time spent fishing each year.

Unfortunately one striking feature of most modern fisheries is the rapid changes that are taking place. Larger and more powerful ships are being built; the trawl nets, purse seines, and other gear are becoming larger and more complex, while a variety of electronic and other auxiliary devices—echo-sounders, sonar netsondes on the trawl, advanced navigational equipment—enable the fishermen to find the fish more easily, and concentrate on the most fruitful grounds. Possibly even more significant, and certainly more difficult to measure or qualify, is the fact that the fishermen themselves are changing. The picture of the fisherman as a traditionalist fishing with the methods and at the times and in the places that his father and grandfather did is out of date, not only in the advanced countries but in Africa, Asia, and Latin America as well. These changing attitudes have been forced on them by the introduction of the new, advanced, and expensive equipment, but has often been helped by improved training schemes—for instance one of the most successful projects in fisheries run by the F.A.O. under the United Nations Development Programme has been for training fishermen in Korea. Some hundreds of graduates from this scheme are now commanding Korean tuna vessels in all parts of the world.

Some of these effects can be measured and appropriate corrections made. Thus the catches of large and small ships can be compared—often catches of trawlers are closely proportional to the tonnage or horsepower of the vessel (Gulland, 1956). If the main change in a fleet of trawlers is an increase in average size, then expressing the fishing effort as, say, the sum of the tonnage of each trawler multiplied by the days it spent at sea, rather than simply as the total days at sea, will provide a satisfactory measure that is consistent from year to year.

While gross changes in the size of ship or in the type of gear can be determined, either by analysing catches of vessels of different sizes under normal commercial conditions, or by direct experimental comparison under controlled conditions—e.g., the ships fishing alongside each other—this is not true of the more subtle changes, particularly the use of equipment to detect and locate the fish more easily.

The more successful items of such equipment are often adopted by the fleet very quickly after being introduced, so that there is only a short transition period during which catches of ships with and without the equipment can be compared. During this period the better fishermen will almost certainly adopt the new equipment first. The effect of the gear will, therefore, be confounded (in the statistical sense) with the efforts of the individual fishermen. The comparison will give at least an upper limit of the effect of the gear, but since the differences between good and poor fishermen is very large (the top skipper will often catch twice the average, and more in some fisheries) this upper limit is likely to be so high as to be of little use.

While strictly quantitative analysis of the effect of many types of improvement in fishing techniques (including changes in the average skill of the fishermen) often cannot be easily made, a more subjective estimation of changes in the fishing power of the fleet may not be too difficult. The fishermen themselves will have a very good idea of the value of new equipment, and the amount they are prepared to pay for it should give a lower limit to its value (though to some extent fishermen are like everyone else in following the latest fashion). The best estimate, if not one immediately expressible in precise quantitative terms will be the simplest—that obtained by asking the fishermen themselves—assuming the question is asked in a civilized fashion over a pint of beer, by someone the fisherman can respect, and who clearly understands what the fishery is about.

Close contact with the fishery is also essential to determine the best measure of fishing time when the patterns of fishing are changing. Under constant conditions any convenient measure can be used—number of trips, days at sea—but just as modern technology has made the gear more efficient once the ship is in contact with the fish, so it has enabled a larger proportion of the time to be spent actively fishing, rather than steaming to and from the grounds, looking for the best place to fish, or stopped by bad weather—a modern stern trawler which shoots and hauls her gear head to wind can work in appreciably worse weather than a traditional side trawler of comparable size which has to turn broadside to the weather to work her gear.

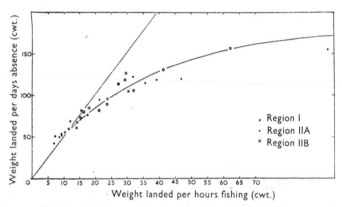

Fig. 12.—Relation between stock abundance, as estimated from catch per hour fishing, and the landings per day at sea. (*From* Gulland, 1956.)

For trawlers the obvious measure of fishing time is the time that the gear is actually on the bottom fishing, and this has been adopted as the general standard, replacing the more easily measured units such as number of trips and days at sea. These latter become particularly unsatisfactory when the proportion of the total time spent actively fishing depends on the abundance of fish—when catches are good fishing may be held up while the crew handle the fish, or the hold is quickly filled so that proportionally more time during the trip is spent steaming to and from the grounds. Then the catch per trip and catch per day at sea will tend to reach an asymptote, and not increase proportionally with the abundance of the stock (*Fig.* 12, from Gulland, 1956).

Any plot of catch per unit effort against effort must be treated with some reserve, and with the suspicion that the unit of fishing effort used may not have remained constant throughout the period of analysis. Almost certainly the change will be that the effectiveness of a unit of effort has increased. Thus, relative to the earlier years, the later data will have the effort too low, and the c.p.u.e. too high. The pattern of modern fishing means that these points will almost certainly be those at the higher levels of effort (on any scale).

The general effects of these changes are shown in *Fig. 13*. The first is that the decline in c.p.u.e., as a proportionate decrease from the unfished level, is likely to be underestimated—i.e., that the stock is being more heavily fished than would appear from the catch records, since the decline may have been masked to a greater or lesser extent by an increase in efficiency of the fleet. However,

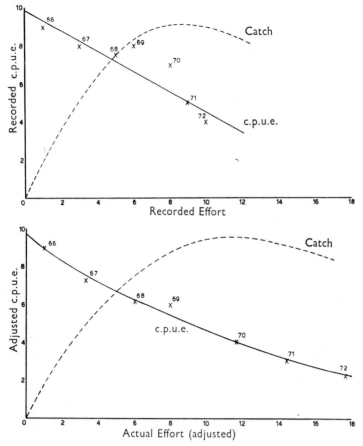

Fig. 13.—Hypothetical example of the effect of changes in fishery efficiency on the estimated relations between amount of fishing and catch and catch per unit effort.

because the true increase in fishing effort has also been under-estimated, the effect on the estimated relation between effort and c.p.u.e., and hence between catch and effort, is complex. If the apparent c.p.u.e. has not decreased much, the immediate con-clusions—that fishing is not affecting the stock, and increased fishing would give approximately proportional increase in catch—are too optimistic. On the other hand, if the apparent c.p.u.e. has decreased greatly, suggesting a heavily fished stock, the conclusion that catastrophic declines in catch are likely from any appreciable further increase in the amount of fishing are probably too pessi-mistic, and the curves of c.p.u.e. or catch against effort are probably flatter than the nominal effort data suggest (*Fig.* 13).

Since the effort in the most recent period is underestimated, the reduction in effort required to return to some desired previous level will be also underestimated, and so also will be the possible benefits in terms of reduced costs. The latter are often potentially the biggest source of profit from managing a fishery—commonly the total catch cannot be changed much. The fact that the estimates of such potential benefits obtained from the present type of catch-effort analysis are likely to be lower limits to the true values is significant when deciding on possible management action.

FURTHER APPLICATIONS TO DATA

While the Schaefer-type model is now normally applied by plotting c.p.u.e. against effort, there are occasions when the net rate of natural increase can be analysed directly. This is best done when the stock size is known at distinct moments—preferably at fixed intervals, such as a year. Occasionally such measurements can be made. For example most of the population of grey whales pass close inshore off San Diego on their way south to the breeding lagoons along the Mexican coast. As they go south they can be counted by observers on shore. Some corrections are made for those passing at night, or too far offshore to be seen, and the difference on successive annual counts gives an estimate of the rate of change in population. Technological advances, such as new acoustic methods with which it is becoming possible to make direct counts of the numbers (and hopefully also some measure of the size) of fish within the beam of the echo-sounder, may enable direct counts of fish stocks to be made more easily in the future.

For the present, however, the abundance of most populations has to be estimated indirectly, particularly from catch and effort data. These rarely give estimates at an instant of time, and usually the catch per unit effort is calculated over a period of a year. This makes it difficult to calculate immediately the change in population between, say, 1 January, 1970, and 1 January, 1971, and relate this to the conditions in 1970.

A technique has been developed by Schaefer (1957) in which the abundance on 1 January, 1970, is computed as the mean of the average abundance in 1969 and 1970. A similar method was applied by the Special Committee of Three Scientists set up by the International Whaling Commission to study the blue whale population (Chapman, 1964). *Fig.* 3, adapted from their report, shows the net rate of national increase (estimated as the difference between the catch and the observed decrease in the stock), plotted as a function of abundance. The scatter is very great, but it is clear, as demanded by general theory, that the increase is small for small stocks, and any fitted curve must pass close to the origin. (Theoretically the curve could cut the horizontal axis to the right of the origin, if at some very small population the reproductive rate falls off because, for example, male and female whales have difficulty in finding each other.)

If it is also accepted, on theoretical grounds, that the curve must cut the axis again at a point corresponding to the unexploited population occurring in, say, 1900, and that the curve is smooth, without marked discontinuities, then the shape of the curve becomes quite well-defined. The line in *Fig.* 3 has been drawn by eye, but clearly no very marked divergence from it could be consistent with the observed data. In particular it is clear that the maximum net rate of increase (equal to the maximum sustained yield) is around 6000 whales per year, and occurs at a population abundance of around 100,000–125,000 animals. The abundance at which the maximum occurs is almost certainly greater than half the unexploited abundance, which is the level suggested by the simple logistic model.

While application of the technique to the blue whales was successful, the application to most fish stocks raises a number of practical difficulties. In the whale population the main change in population was the fishery-induced decline. The animals are long-lived, and the survival of young differs little from year to year, and the actual change in population in any year is almost exactly the difference between the catch and the average net rate of increase for the current population size. The deviations from the line (which are not inconsiderable) are mostly due to the difficulties in estimating abundance, which are exaggerated when considering the changes in estimated abundance from one year to the next.

In contrast to whale populations most fish populations vary quite considerably even in the absence of fishing, particularly owing to changes in year-class abundance. These fluctuations mean that the actual change in stock abundance during any year may depend as much on the variation in the strength of year-classes present as on the difference between the catch and the average net rate of natural increase (sustainable yield) for the current level of abundance. Thus when a strong year-class enters the fishery there is almost bound to be an increase in abundance, whatever the catch, followed by a decline when the fish of good year-class become old and most have died. Year-class fluctuations will add greatly to the scatter of points in any plot of net change in population against abundance. Also, as pointed out by Gulland (1968), these complicate the simpler concepts of sustainable yield. Several concepts can be distinguished. In one, the sustainable yield for any year is that which leaves the population at the end of the year the same as it was at the beginning. Another, as outlined above, equates the sustainable yield to the net rate of natural increase, or, more precisely, to the net rate of increase for populations of the current abundance, under average conditions. A slightly more sophisticated version of the second concept, which is described in more detail in the following sections, is that the sustainable yield is that yield that would be obtained by the fishing mortality which, under average conditions, would result in a stock abundance equal to that observed. Specifically, under average conditions there may be some fishing mortality which maintained over a long period gives the greatest yield. For any one year, the maximum sustained yield might then be considered as the yield that would be obtained by exerting that fishing mortality.

Clearly, if conditions do not vary other than due to the direct effects of fishing, these definitions are equivalent. This is not so if conditions vary. Thus in the case of the haddock stocks on Georges Bank, off New England, there were two successive strong year-classes, those of 1962 and 1963, which entered the fishery in 1965/66. Although these fish were extremely heavily exploited, both by local vessels and Russian long-range trawlers, the stock abundance actually increased between 1964 and 1967. Conversely, after 1967, when the later, and rather poor year-class were coming into the fishery, the stock declined, even though the amount of fishing had become only moderate, with the diversion of the Russian fleet to other stocks. In fact in some of the later years when most of fish were the old survivors of the 1962 and 1963 year-classes, which were growing very slowly, and the incoming year-class was very poor, the stock might have declined even if there had been no fishing. Under one definition this would imply a negative sustainable yield for that year.

Another, and theoretically important, objection to the simple approach is that it takes no account of the time-lags in the system. The natural rate of increase in weight of the exploited part of the stock is made up of two parts—the growth of the individuals already present, and the recruitment of young fish reaching a catchable size. The first of these is clearly directly related to the current abundance, though it may also be influenced by the abundance in previous years—the more fish in the previous year, the less the abundance of the food supply, hence the slower the growth. Also the age-composition will affect the growth; for example, young haddock newly recruited to the Georges Bank stock may double in weight in a year, and if they are the main constituent of the stock the average growth rate for the stock as a whole may be around 50 per cent. On the other hand, if most of the fish are old, as has been the case lately, the overall gross increase due to growth may be as little as 10–20 per cent.

The number of recruits is clearly most related to the abundance of the stock (or the mature part of the stock) at the time the fish were born, rather than at the time they recruited. The age at recruitment can vary from a few months in the case of shrimp, to a couple of years for haddock, and up to ten years for halibut. In the blue whale analysis above, where the population abundance was expressed in numbers, and the only cause of natural increase was recruitment, the problem of time-lags was dealt with by relating the net increase in one year to the abundance four years previously. At the time the analysis was made four years was believed to be the age of recruitment, though this is now believed to be an underestimate. However, the year-to-year changes in abundance of blue whales were not sufficient for this discrepancy seriously to affect the analysis. For most fish stock the lags in different parts of the system—growth, recruitment, and mortality —are probably sufficiently different for it to be difficult to make corrections in this way.

These difficulties over time-lags are one aspect of the fundamental disadvantage of the simple, or Schaefer-type, approach, compared with the more complex analytic, or Ricker or Beverton and Holt, approaches described later. Once the simple analysis has been made of the basic catch and effort data it is extremely difficult to use additional data, on for example the age at recruitment, or fluctuation of year-class strengths, to improve the accuracy of the estimates obtained.

Unless conditions are exceptionally favourable to the scientist any analysis, in the form of, say, a plot of catch per unit effort against effort, will reveal a degree of scatter, often quite high. Commonly this variation will allow fairly broad conclusions to be drawn about the state of the stock, perhaps showing that it is being heavily exploited and that some management action is likely to be useful. However, it may not be so clear what the precise action should be; as regards, for example, the level of the maximum sustainable yield or the optimum amount of fishing. It can be hoped that the passage of time, by adding further points—though generally at the rate of only one per year—will allow the relation between effort and catch (or catch per unit effort) to be determined more precisely. Unfortunately the improvement in precision achieved in this way from adding further points to the graph becomes very slow after a few years. Also after a period some of the conditions, other than the amount of fishing, may change. The points corresponding to the early period could then be rather irrelevant to the later situation; so far as giving advice for management of the current fishery is concerned, in some circumstances little improvement can be achieved from having a larger series of simple catch and effort data, without taking into account other changes that have occurred.

These changes may include both natural changes, such as the gradual warming of the water of West Greenland during the first half of this century, which allowed a great increase in the abundance and extent of the cod stocks, and changes in the pattern of fishing, other than simply in the amount of fishing. Thus in the yellowfin tuna fishery in the eastern tropical Pacific there was a revolution in the method of fishing in the late 1950s. The traditional method of pole-and-line fishing with live bait was rather suddenly replaced by purse-seining. This change increased the effective fishing power of the existing vessels, and to the building of successively larger super-seiners capable of carrying a thousand tons of frozen tuna, and using ever larger and more efficient nets.

In addition the size of fish caught was changed. Tuna of different sizes tend to swim at different depths, with the smallest

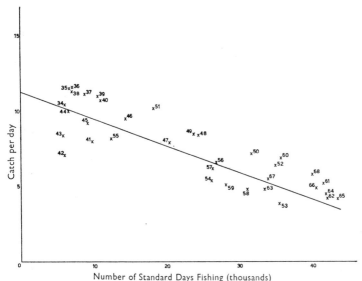

Fig. 14.—Relation between the catch of yellowfin tuna per days fishing, in standard units, in the Estern Tropical Pacific, and the total fishing effort. The line is fitted to the points up to and including 1959. (*Adapted from* I.A.T.T.C. reports.)

at the top. It was these small fish at the surface which were mainly caught by the pole-and-line fishermen. The purse-seine, and particularly the newest and largest nets, will catch all the fish in the school, including the larger and deeper swimming animals. As is shown in the following sections, the same catch, or the same effort, will have different effects on the stock, and on future catches, depending on the sizes of fish taken. At high rates of exploitation, the capture of large fish, which allows the smaller fish to grow, will result in appreciably larger sustained catches. As a result the points corresponding to recent yellowfin fishing tend to lie progressively above the straight line fitted to the early data (*Fig.* 14).

The divergence between this line, and the more recent points is increased by other factors. The seiners are moving farther west into areas untouched in the early period, and may be exploiting a rather larger stock; also the true relation between effort and catch per unit is probably not a straight line, but is curved upward. The last effect can be taken into account by the simple model without requiring more than further annual series of catch and effort data. The others can only be dealt with by introducing the more complex analytic ideas. These ideas are likely, therefore, to have to be used in all but the most simple situations, or those in which only the simplest data are yet available.

ANALYTIC MODELS

These models consider the population of fish as the sum of its individual members, rather than as a single unit, and analyse the growth and death of these individuals. The basic axiom is that all fish die once but only once. In the simpler models assumptions are made that the rate of growth, the death-rates from causes other than fishing, and the number of young fish recruiting to the fishery each year are constant and independent of the abundance of the stock or the amount of fishing. It is also normally assumed that the individual fish of the same age do not differ among themselves as regards their rate of growth, susceptibility to capture by various fishing gear, etc. All these assumptions can be relaxed and replaced by more realistic, though more complex, models as the situation demands, and as more data become available to use such models.

The analysis is usually approached by considering the history of a cohort of fish from the time they reach a fishable size until they are all dead. Clearly, under given steady conditions of fishing and other factors, the average yield in a year from all year-classes present will be equal to the yield from any one year-class during its life. During any interval of time an individual fish can either be caught, die of natural causes, or survive to the beginning of the next period. These survivors can therefore be calculated as the difference between the number alive at the beginning of the period, and the deaths during the period. These deaths can be calculated as functions of the fishing and natural mortalities. The catch in weight during the interval will be equal to the product of the numbers caught and their average weight, which is easily known if the time interval is short, so that there is not much growth. The total catch is then obtained by addition of the catches in the individual time intervals. That is, the yield Y, can be written:

$$Y = \sum_r W_r P_r N_r$$

where W_r is the average weight of fish caught in the rth interval and P_r is the proportion of the N_r fish alive at the beginning of the rth interval, which are caught during that interval.

The main assumption that has to be made in using this approach concerns the death-rates. The first step is essentially a matter of definition, rather than assumption. Coefficients of fishing and natural mortality (F and M respectively), may be defined as the instantaneous rates of death from the two causes, such that for a cohort of N individual fish in a very short interval of time, dt

deaths due to fishing (the catch) = FNdt,
deaths due to other causes   = MNdt.

A further definition is of fishing effort as the amount of fishing, measured in such appropriate units that it will be proportional to the fishery mortality. The assumption then has to be made that the best nominal units of fishing effort that are available, e.g., numbers of hours fishing by trawlers of a standard size, are in fact acceptable units of effort, and are proportional to the fishing mortality, that is, denoting the recorded fishing effort as f, a basic assumption is that $F = qf$, where q is a constant, sometimes referred to as the 'catchability coefficient'.

As discussed previously, the degree to which the units of fishing effort available (e.g., number of voyages, the sum of the products of the hours fishing times the gross tonnage of the vessel concerned) actually measure the true amount of fishing—i.e., the extent to which the value of q remains unchanged over a period—is a central problem of fishery research. While no available effort unit is entirely perfect, and many depart quite widely from perfection, for nearly all fisheries there exists some effort unit which will give a reasonable measure of fishing mortality, and which used in the calculation catch per unit effort, will provide a more satisfactory index of abundance than any other readily available.

A number of other assumptions have, as already mentioned, to be made to enable the model to be developed in any simple form. These assumptions, e.g., that the pattern of growth does not change, and that the natural mortality coefficient is the same for fish of different ages, and is unchanged from year to year—are generally entirely reasonable as first approximations.

The actual calculations, if they are to be expressed in a simple algebraic form, also require a convenient mathematical expression for the growth of the individual fish. The algebra is easier if the expression for growth can be combined easily with the expression for the numbers of fish. The latter can be obtained from the mortality rates, since, in mathematical terms, the rate of change of numbers is given by

$$\frac{dN}{dt} = -FN - MN = -ZN$$

where $Z = F + M =$ total mortality coefficient. If Z is constant, this is a simple differential equation, which can be reasily solved to give

$$N = N_0 e^{-Zt}$$

where $N_0 =$ number of fish alive at time $t = 0$, that is the numbers decline at a constant exponential rate.

The most convenient expression for growth to combine with this is therefore a constant exponential growth rate. This has been used by Ricker (1958), in the form $W_t = W_0 e^{gt}$. A constant exponential growth is unrealistic if used over a wide range of ages. The growth of young fish often fits an exponential pattern for a period, but then the growth slows down. A better fit can readily be obtained by dividing the life span into a number of intervals, in each of which growth is more closely exponential, though at different rates. Simple mathematics can then show that the yield in weight from the first interval, from time 0 to T, is given by

$$Y = \frac{FN_0W_0}{g-Z}(e^{-(g-Z)T} - 1)$$

and similar expressions can be derived for other intervals.

Another expression which gives a fit over a wider range of ages is the von Bertalanffy growth curve, used by Beverton and Holt (1957). This expresses the weight in the form

$$W_t = W_\infty(1 - e^{-K(t-t_0)})^3$$

which, when combined with the expression for numbers, provides the expression for the yield

$$Y = FRW_\infty \sum_{n=0}^{3} \frac{U_n e^{-nK(t_r - t_0)}}{F + M + nK}$$

where $U_0 = 1$, $U_1 = -3$, $U_2 = 3$, $U_3 = -1$; $t_r =$ age at recruitment, i.e. the age at which the fish enter the fishery and first become accessible to fishing gear, and $R =$ number of recruits, i.e., the number alive at the age of recruitment.

In many fisheries the fish do not begin to be caught immediately after recruitment, but the smaller recruited fish are protected, possible by a deliberate management policy such as the use of large meshes in trawls. This is expressed most simply by assuming that fishing mortality is zero up to some age, the age at first capture—usually denoted by t_c—and thereafter assumes its full, constant, value. Then the yield will be given by

$$Y = FRW_\infty e^{-M(t_c - t_r)} \sum \frac{U_n e^{-nK(t_c - t_0)}}{F + M + nK}$$

For the present purposes the exact form of these expressions is unimportant. The essential point is that the yield can be determined for any combination of the amount of fishing (F), and the age at first capture (t_c).

To make the calculation it is necessary to have estimates of the several parameters in the equation for the yield. The parameters relating to the growth of the individual fish (W_∞, K, t_0) are easily calculated if, as commonly occurs, the age of the individual fish can be determined, e.g., from scales or otoliths. The pattern of growth plus some knowledge of the general biology and behaviour of the fish can provide an estimate for the age at recruitment, t_r.

For purposes of calculation and exposition a range of values of the age at first capture, t_c, can be used without further analysis, but for considering management the characteristics of the fishery (e.g., the mesh size of trawls or the area or season of fishing) necessary to achieve a particular age at first capture needs to be established. Similarly, theoretical calculations can be made for a range of values of fishing mortality, F, which have then, if they are to have practical significance to those concerned with management, to be interpreted in terms of the amount of fishing or nominal fishing effort.

The natural mortality coefficient, M, is difficult to estimate directly. Usually only the total mortality, Z, is easily measured, and various techniques are used to separate this between fishing and natural mortality. Since the conclusion about the effect of management measures can depend quite critically on the value of the natural mortality—if it is high it is worth catching them while you can, while if it is low it will be worthwhile to reduce the amount of fishing to allow the fish to grow—it is often desirable to repeat the calculations for a number of values of the natural mortality.

The last parameter is the recruitment, R, which is often not explicitly estimated, but rather the yield expressed as the yield per recruit, Y/R. There are a number of reasons for this. The first is that the recruitment is difficult to estimate directly, and in many fisheries the best estimate is obtained by calculating, from the estimated values of the other parameters, the yield per recruit, and obtaining the value of the recruitment by dividing this into the observed value of the yield. Calculating yield, rather than yield per recruit, therefore, often involves a circular argument, and adds nothing to the information required for management. Another reason is that in a number of fisheries, especially in temperate or sub-arctic waters—e.g., the haddock stock in the North Sea—the annual recruitment fluctuates very widely in a manner that is apparently essentially random and quite independent of fishing. In these fisheries it is quite impossible to predict more than a year or so in advance what the yield in a particular year, for a given pattern of fishing, is likely to be. It is possible to predict the yield per recruit, and, more important, to compare the yields per recruit for different patterns of fishing. Thus it can be shown, for example, that for the North Sea haddock the yield per recruit for a given level of fishing would be increased by say, 10 per cent, by increasing the mesh size in use from 70 mm. to 80 mm. If this change is made, the actual yield in the years following might be above or below the previous yields depending on the strength of the incoming year-classes. The important point is that, after a transition period, the yields would—at least in the simple theory—be 10 per cent greater than they would have been if the mesh change had not been made. In general, the advice from the population analysis is most useful when comparing the results of different management actions (including the results of taking no explicit action).

Another, and in many ways, the most important reason for expressing the results as yield per recruit is that the least satisfactory assumption made in the simple model is that the average recruitment is unaffected by the amount of fishing, or by the abundance of the parent stock. In practice the relation between stock and recruitment can take many forms, which have very different effects on the form of the curve of total yield against amount of fishing. Also it is difficult to estimate what the true form of the curve is for a particular stock of fish—*see*, for example, the discussions at the Symposium on Stock and Recruitment held at Aarhus in 1970 (Larkin and Parrish, 1973).

It is therefore useful to give a fairly explicit warning of these difficulties by expressing the results as yield per recruit. A range of stock-recruit relations can then be incorporated, and the implications of these compared.

The result of these calculations give the yield per recruit (or yield) as a function of two independent variables, which are in principle controllable by suitable management action—the fishing mortality, F, and the age at first capture t_c. These results can be best presented in a two-dimensional diagram, in which the yield from any combination of F and t_c can be easily read off (*see Fig. 6*).

The formulation of yield in the equation above is the most widely used expression in explicit mathematical terms. Calculations that take into account more complex growth curves, or variations of fishing mortality with age, can now be readily made with a computer, dividing the life span into short periods in each of which the various parameters change little. These calculations can become extremely lengthy, as more and more information becomes available.

Those relating to biological aspects, such as the inclusion of a seasonal pattern of growth, rather than a uniform growth throughout the year, will add to the realism and precision of the results, but introduce no essential new concepts, and will not be discussed further. It is also possible to introduce operational or economic complications. Thus not only can the fishing mortality vary accordingly with the season, and with the size or age of fish, but the cost of exerting a certain level of fishing mortality is likely to vary with the season. Also the value of the catch can vary with the season or age of fish. In many fisheries a medium-sized fish fetches a noticeably better price per pound than a small fish, and often rather better than a big fish, while both market demand and changes in the condition of the fish will impose a seasonal pattern.

These and other complexities are in principle easily incorporated in a computer calculation. Thus the equation for the yield in weight can be rewritten in economic terms, and including the effects of both age and season, as

$$\text{Yield in value} = \sum_{t=0}^{T} \sum_{r=1}^{R} V_{r,t} \times W_{r,t} \times P_{r,t} \times N_{r,t}$$

where the year has been divided into R seasons, and T is the maximum age of the fish, $P_{r,t}$ is the proportion of fish age t alive at the beginning of the rth season which are caught in that season, and $V_{r,t}$ denotes the price per pound of fish aged t during the rth season, which will include the effects of the size of fish and of the season, also the cost of fishing can be written as,

$$\text{cost} = \sum c_r f_r$$

where f_r = fishing effort during the rth season

c_r = cost of exerting one unit of fish effort during the rth season

also taking into account possible variations of the effectiveness of a unit of effort at different seasons, and on different ages of fish, the fishing mortality on fish age t can be written as

$$F_{r,t} = q_{r,t} f_r.$$

The values of p and N can be derived from the mortality rates, using the exponential forms derived earlier, but if the time intervals are short, so that the change in population numbers during an interval is small, approximations can be used, i.e., catch $= F_{r,t} N_{r,t} r$, where r = duration of r season; natural deaths $= M_{r,t} N_{r,t} r$

$$N_{r+1,t} = N_{r,t} (1 - F_{r,t} r - M_{r,t} r) \qquad r < R$$
$$N_{1,t+1} = N_{R,t} (1 - F_{Rt} R - M_{R,t} R) \qquad r = R$$

and these can easily be used in a computer to give in succession the numbers caught in each period.

FURTHER BIOLOGICAL FACTORS

The analytical models described in the previous section considered only the immediate and direct effects of fishing on the population. In the first instance fishing will only alter the rate at which fish are dying; their growth rate and the numbers of recruits will not be directly affected. However, it is obvious that as fish are removed by man there will probably be more food available for the survivors, which may grow faster and may also suffer a lower mortality from food shortage or disease. On the other hand fewer adult fish may well mean that fewer young are produced.

In principle these effects can be incorporated into the simple models without much modification of the basic concepts. Instead of treating, say, all the growth parameters as constant, one or more may be considered as a function of the abundance of the stock. For instance, using the von Bertalanffy growth curve, the limiting weight W_∞ can be written as a linear function of the total biomass, B, of the population

$$W_\infty = a - bB$$

and the biomass itself, can, using the same techniques as used in calculating the yield, be expressed as a function of the fishing mortality, W_∞, and the other parameters. It is then a matter of more or less complex computation to determine the growth parameters, and hence the yield, for any given fishing mortality. Essentially the same procedure can be followed when considering the indirect effects of fishing on other growth parameters, or on natural mortality or recruitment.

So far as management is concerned the important question is what effect the incorporation of these additional factors has on the relation between the amount of the fishing and the yield. Several studies of this have been made, especially by Beverton and Holt (1957).

Changes in growth cause fewest problems. Since the growth of invididual fish is often quite easy to determine, the effect of density on growth, if it is at all significant, can be readily measured, and the results duly incorporated in the calculation. For example, *Fig.* 15 shows the reduction in growth of haddock in the North Sea during their second year of life as a result of increased abundance; *Fig.* 16 shows the effect of incorporating this density-dependent growth in the curve relating yield to fishing effort (*from* Beverton and Holt, 1957). The revised curve is flatter, with a less pronounced maximum, and one which occurs at a very slightly higher fishing mortality. The differences are not ones that would seriously affect management decisions—both curves show quite clearly that the fishing mortality of 0·7, which has been exerted for a long time, is much too high.

Density-dependent changes in natural mortality have much the same, moderately flattening effect. Where in the simple model a change in fishing would result in a big fall in stock abundance, the reduced stock might suffer a smaller natural death-rate, and hence a less marked fall in abundance would occur. It is therefore likely that it is not very important to take density-dependent changes in natural mortality into account when preparing the scientific evidence for management action since the changes that would occur would be in the same direction as those predicted on the basis of a constant natural mortality, but of a slightly smaller magnitude. This is fortunate because natural mortality and, still more, changes in it, are difficult to measure and to relate to changes in stock abundance.

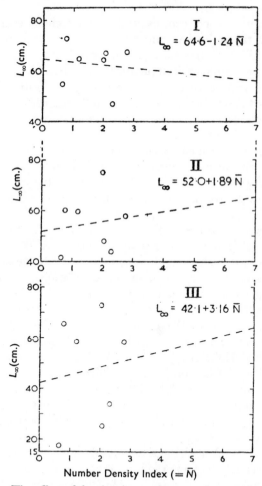

Fig. 15.—The effect of density, in numbers, on the growth of haddock of age I, II, and III, in the eastern area of the North Sea, as indicated by the estimated limiting length L_∞. (*From* Beverton and Holt, 1957.)

DENSITY-DEPENDENT RECRUITMENT

Changes in the number of recruits present the biggest scientific problem in many management situations. The relationship between the recruitment and the abundance of the present stock is difficult to determine; but the precise form of this relationship

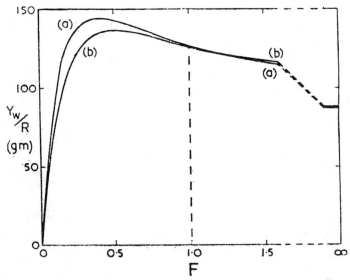

Fig. 16.—The yield curve of North Sea haddock with (curve b) and without (curve a) taking into account the effect of density dependent growth. (*From* Beverton and Holt, 1957.)

can have a very critical influence on the shape of the yield/effort curve and hence on management decisions.

The management difficulties are well illustrated by those met in the world's biggest fishery. After an explosive development, during which annual catches increased from some 100,000 tons in 1956 to over 8 million tons in 1964, the Peruvian anchovy fishery has been limited by a variety of Government measures to some 8–10 million tons per year. The declared purpose of these measures has always been to conserve the stock of fish, though the acceptability of the regulations has often been helped by the market situation. Though demand for fish meal has steadily increased, e.g. through the spread of battery-rearing of chickens, the rapid increase of the Peruvian production—a doubling each year of the output from what soon became the world's

95

biggest producer, had tended to be more than the market could absorb. Restriction of output therefore gave a welcome support to prices that might otherwise have fallen sharply—or more sharply than they actually did. Fish meal manufacturers, like anyone else, are most willing to act for the benefit of future fisheries when the act is to their short-term advantage.

The Peruvian anchovy fishery has, through its sheer size, and also by the good series of basic statistical data that are available, attracted attention from a large proportion of the limited world stock of fish population experts, particularly through the United Nations Development Programmes operated in Peru by the F.A.O. The analysis was in the first instance made on the basis of the direct catch and effort data, using a simple Schaefer-type approach. Later analyses have been more complex, taking into account more factors of the life history of the anchoveta. These have not altered the early conclusions very much, but still leave some important questions unanswered. It is clear that fishing had reached, by 1967, a level at which total catches increased only slowly with increased amounts of fishing. The yield per recruit would be expected to continue to increase, though slowly, for increases in effort considerably beyond the present. However, the adult stock would decrease. If this decrease caused a decrease in recruitment, then increases in effort would, if continued, result in a sharp drop in total catch. On the other hand, it is not impossible since young and old anchoveta may be competing for the same food, that a decrease in adult stock, if not too severe, could actually increase the average level of recruitment.

The result is that it is possible, under two different but not unreasonable hypotheses concerning the nature of the stock-recruitment relation, for two very different conclusions to be reached concerning the effect on total catch of a substantial increase in fishing, say, a doubling of the present amount. One predicts that there will be a sharp drop, perhaps to 5 million tons or less; the other predicts a slight increase, from around 10 million tons to perhaps 12 million tons. This difference is not only absolutely critical to the whole industry, but is highly significant for the whole economy of Peru, for which fish meal is one of the biggest earners of foreign exchange.

An uncertainty concerning the stock-recruit relationship and the critical importance of this relation to management decisions—should the fishing effort in Peru be allowed (or even encouraged) to increase much beyond the present level ?—is not limited to the anchoveta. The whole subject was recently reviewed at a symposium at the University of Aarhus, Denmark, organized by the International Council for the Exploration of the Sea (Larkin and Parrish, 1973). It is clear that only for a minority of stocks can the shape of the stock-recruit curve be determined with any degree of precision.

The reasons for this failure are several. There is no clear agreement on what the precise shape of the curve should be, though it is clearly, at least at lower levels of stock, curved, possibly sharply. There is a wide choice in the degree of curvature, and the point at which the relation begins to depart significantly from a straight line. This makes fitting an empirical curve to the data much harder than if a straight line had been a reasonable theoretical representation. Empirical fitting is also difficult because there is usually a great deal of variation in annual recruitment for reasons that seem quite independent of changes in adult stock, and only one point, of a pair of values of adult stock and subsequent recruitment, becomes available each year.

The implications of any particular stock-recruit relation on the relation between total yield and amount of fishing can be derived from the stock-recruit curve, and the yield per recruit relation obtained from the simple constant parameter equation set out in the earlier section. The first step is to solve two simultaneous equations for stock and recruits, one giving the recruitment from a given stock and the other the adult stock which would result from a given recruitment and a given pattern of fishing, using the calculations based on growth and natural and fishing mortality described earlier. If wished, density-dependent growth and natural mortality effects can be included in the latter equation. The solution is readily done, and most easily understood, graphically, as shown in *Fig.* 17.

This figure shows, as the curved line, a typical stock-recruit curve; the relation between recruitment and resulting stock will be a straight line (unless effects of density-dependent growth and mortality are included) whose slope will depend on the pattern of fishing. The point **A** where the line cuts the curve is the solution to the equations. It gives the magnitude of the recruitment that will occur for the given pattern of fishing under equilibrium conditions. This can be incorporated in the earlier expression of yield per recruit to give the actual yield.

The calculations can be repeated for any other pattern of fishing. As the amount of fishing increases, the adult stock resulting from a given recruitment will decrease. That is, as the line is drawn in the figure, the slope of it will increase. The effect of an increased amount of fishing is shown in *Fig.* 18. Under light fishing the stock has stabilized at the position **P**. With increased fishing the new recruitment-stock relation is the steeper line **OP¹**. This gives the new equilibrium position **P¹**, but the population will not reach

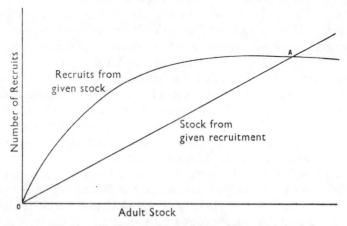

Fig. 17.—The equilibrium position of a stock in which recruitment is density dependent, determined by the intersection of the given stock-recruit curve, with the straight line relation between recruitment and the resulting stock.

this position immediately, rather proceeding to it in stages, as shown in the figure. The old recruitment will give a reduced adult stock, S_1, when the horizontal line through **P** cuts the new line; from this stock, S_1, a number of recruits, R_1, will result, which in turn will produce a stock, S_2, and so on.

It may be seen that this converging movement to an equilibrium position can apply equally to the recovery from any type of disturbance, and not merely a fishery-induced change. The stock-recruit relation, therefore, provided that it is of a suitable shape, provides a mechanism for the stability of the population.

The effect of incorporating a density-dependent recruitment into the calculation of the yield curve will depend on the shape of the curve. If, as is not unlikely, it is of the same general shape as that shown in *Fig.* 17—with recruitment not changing much at moderate to high stocks, but decreasing at lower stocks—the result will be to sharpen any peaks in the curve, and also to increase the benefits to be expected from any restrictive measures, such as a reduction in the amount of fishing or an increase in the size at first capture. These changes in the shape of the yield curve become more pronounced the more there are significant decreases in recruitment at levels of population size that are likely to occur at moderately heavy levels of fishing.

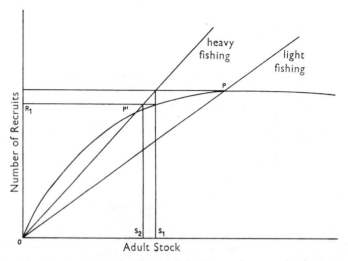

Fig. 18.—The transitional changes following an increase in the amount of fishing, illustrating the stabilizing effect of the stock-recruit curve.

The result of using different relations, as shown in *Fig.* 19 (*from* Gulland, 1968) in which are shown (*above*) two curves of total yield against amount of fishing in the Peruvian anchoveta fishery. The full line shows the relation obtained if it is assumed that recruitment remains constant, at least for sizes of adult stock likely to be obtained with any practicable amounts of fishing; the broken curve illustrates a stock-recruit curve similar to that in *Fig.* 16, in which the recruitment has a maximum at a fairly high stock, and begins to decrease appreciably at only moderately small stocks. The curves have been drawn to coincide at the present level of fishing. As already noted they predict very different results of increasing the amount of fishing substantially beyond the present level (*Fig.* 19, *overleaf*). The broken curve in the upper figure was chosen to result in the Schaefer-type parabolic relation between fishing and the total yield shown in the lower figure.

While it is not yet possible to distinguish between these possibilities in the Peruvian anchoveta, and there are similar difficulties in other stocks, some progress is being made toward understanding the problem, as described in the proceedings of the Aarhus Symposium. Thus, while the precise shape of the curve cannot

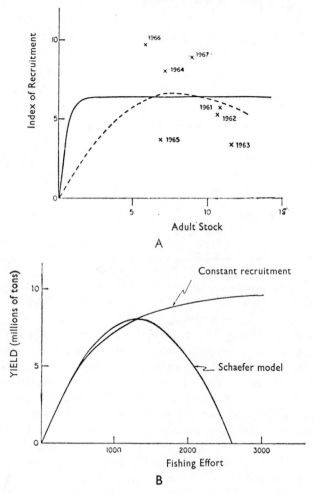

Fig. 19.—The stock-recruitment relation in the Peruvian anchovy, showing possible relations (**A**) and their influence on the yield curve (**B**). (*From* Gulland, 1968.)

be predicted some general shapes have been predicted. Ricker (1954) suggested on the basis of theoretical assumptions on the density-dependent mortality among the young, pre-recruit fish, a curve with a maximum at moderate stocks, such as that of *Fig.* 16, and this has been shown to fit several stocks, especially the salmon in the North Pacific, for which the stock-recruit relation has been studied in some detail. Beverton and Holt (1957), making slightly different assumptions, derived a slightly different relation, with no maximum. Other curves could be derived with other assumptions, but so far for all stocks the observations of stock and recruitment, though often scattered, have been consistent with at least one of the theoretical curves.

The difficulty has been that because of the scatter of points both types of curve could be fitted, and, in the case of the Ricker type, could be fitted with a wide range of alternatives concerning the position and magnitude of the maximum. Cushing and Harris (1973) have shown that there is a fairly consistent pattern within different groups of fish, seemingly related to the numbers of eggs produced by an individual female. For salmon, which produce only a few thousand each, the maximum is pronounced, and occurs at a fairly large stock. As the stock is reduced from the unexploited level the recruitment rises slightly and then falls quite sharply at stock levels which are still quite large. At the other extreme, the stock-recruitment curve for flatfish, which produce hundreds of thousands of eggs per individual adult female, tends to be flat with no pronounced maximum and no significant fall in average recruitment, even when the stock has been reduced to a small fraction of its original level. If these generalizations hold then the management of a fishery on flatfish can afford to pay relatively little attention to the stock-recruit relation and to the need to maintain the stock at the level giving optimum recruitment. In such fisheries management is mainly concerned with optimizing the yield from whatever the recruitment happens to be. In salmon fisheries the biggest problem is likely to be the maintenance of the spawning stock at the level giving optimum recruitment; scientists will be deeply concerned in determining what is the optimum level. This need to maintain an adequate spawning stock is made more critical by the ability of fishermen in the rivers, or near their mouths, to remove, by the use of the most effective types of gears the great majority of spawning salmon attempting to pass upstream. Such fishermen, using for example traps, can, if not restricted, exert a fishing mortality much higher than can normally be exerted with equivalent costs by any high-sea fishery, whether on salmon or other species.

This similarity within groups of species removes some of the uncertainty and thus aids the management of the stocks, but within each group a great deal of variation remains. This variation can be removed only by a better understanding of the processes determining the average recruitment from a given stock. This is due to some form of density-dependent mortality among the pre-recruit fish, probably in the first few weeks of life. If this mortality is proportional to the density of adults, or the initial density of eggs or young, then a Ricker-type curve can be obtained. If the mortality at any instant of time is governed by the current density of young fish, then a Beverton and Holt-type curve can be derived.

Two methods of studying the nature of this mortality are emerging. One is essentially the same as that used to study the older fish. Instead of using the catches of commercial vessels, the abundance of the eggs and larvae can be estimated at successive moments by the catches of research vessels using suitable types of nets (Sette, 1943; Ahlstrom, 1966). The other is to rear young fish in the laboratory and to study their growth, food requirements, and mortality. It seems that, naturally enough, the growth of very young fish depends greatly on the food supply. If there is not enough growth slows down or stops. At certain times, especially when the baby fish has just exhausted the supply of food it is born with in the egg-yolk, lack of food can cause death directly, but in any case a small and weak larva is a much more likely victim to a predator than a strong and well-fed one. To some extent the food supply of a young plaice must depend on the abundance of young plaice—the more there are the more the food will be grazed down. It is therefore not difficult to set up a logical chain of increased parent abundance—more larvae—more grazing—less food—poorer growth—higher mortality—constant or reduced recruitment, in which most of the links could be determined in an independent and quantitative manner. So far such a complete chain, with corresponding estimates of the effects at each stage has not been constructed, but this will probably be done soon and most of the links were described in one or more of the papers at the 1970 Aarhus symposium. Hopefully this or other approaches, separately or in combination, will enable more precise estimates of the stock-recruit relation to be determined for any stock or interest.

For the present and immediate future, however, the relation is likely to remain uncertain for many stocks. This will result in a corresponding uncertainty in the scientific advice given to managers of fisheries. They will, therefore, have to take decisions, in scientific as in many other matters, on a balance of probabilities. One simplifying factor is that, except for those stocks not greatly reduced in abundance below their unexploited level in which the problem of management is unlikely to be acute, the probable direction of any effect of density-dependent recruitment is known. More adults are likely to mean more recruits, so that any assessment of the effects of regulations based on an assumption of constant recruitment will underestimate the subsequent recruitment and therefore yield. If therefore an estimate based on constant recruitment assumption points to the desirability of introducing a certain restrictive measure, then it can be introduced without worrying too much about possible density-dependent recruitment.

REFERENCES

AHLSTROM, E. H. (1966), 'Distribution and abundance of sardine and anchovy larvae in the California current region off California and Baja California, 1951–64. A summary', *U.S. Fish. Wildl. Serv., Spec. Sci. Rept.* **534**, 71.

BARANOV, F. I. (1918), 'On the question of the biological basis of fisheries', *Nauchnyi Issledovatelskii Ikhtiologecheshii Institut Isvestia*, **1**(1), 81–128.

BEVERTON, R. J. H., and HOLT, S. J. (1957), 'On the dynamics of exploited fish populations', *Fish Invest., Lond.*, ser. 2, **19**, 533.

CHAPMAN, D. G. (1964), Final report of the Committee of Three Scientists., *Rep. Int. Whaling Commn.*, **14**, 39–92.

CUSHING, D. H., and HARRIS, J. G. K. (1973), 'Stock and recruitment and the problem of density dependence', *Rapp. Proc. Verb. Cons. int. Explor. Mer*, 163.

GRAHAM, M. (1939), 'The sigmoid curve and the over-fishing problem', *Rapp. Proc. Verb. Cons. Explor. Mer*, **110**(2), 15–20.

GULLAND, J. A. (1956), 'On the fishing effort in English demersal fisheries', *Fish. Invest., Lond.*, ser. 2, **20**(5), 41.

GULLAND, J. A. (1961), 'Fishing and the stocks of fish at Iceland', *Fish. Invest., Lond.*, ser. 2, **23**(4), 52.

GULLAND, J. A. (1968), 'The concept of the maximum sustained yield and fishery management', *F.A.O. Fish. Tech. Pap.*, (70), 13.

GULLAND, J. A. (1969), 'Manual of methods for fish stock assessment. Part I. Fish population analysis', *F.A.O. Man. Fish. Sci.*, (4), 154.

GULLAND, J. A. (1973), 'Can a study of stock and recruitment and management decisions', *Rapp. Proc. Verb. Cons. int. Explor. Mer*, 163.

LARKIN, P. A., and PARRISH, B. B. (ed.) (1973), 'Symposium on Stock and Recruitment', *Rapp. Proc. Verb. Cons. int. Explor. Mer*, 163.

RICKER, W. E. (1948), 'Methods of estimating vital statistics of fish populations', *Bloomington, Indiana Univ. Publ. Sci. Ser.*, (15), 101.

RICKER, W. E. (1954), 'Stock and recruitment', *J. Fish. Res. Bd Can.*, 11(5), 559–623.

RICKER, W. E. (1958), 'Handbook of computations for biological statistics of fish populations', *Bull. Fish. Res. Bd Can.*, 119, 300.

SCHAEFER, M. B. (1954), 'Some aspects of the dynamics of populations important to the management of commerical marine fisheries', *Bull. Inter-Am. Trop. Tuna Commn.*, 1(2), 27–56.

SCHAEFER, M. B. (1957), 'A study of the dynamics of the fishery for yellow fin tuna in the estern tropical Pacific Ocean', *Bull. Inter-Am. Trop. Tuna Commn.*, 2(6), 247–285.

SETTE, O. E. (1943), 'Biology of the Atlantic mackerel (*Scomber scombrus*) of North America', *Fishery Bull. U.S. Fish. Wildl. Serv.*, Pt. I, 50, 149–237.

Chapter

5

THE OBJECTIVES OF MANAGEMENT

EVERYBODY concerned with fishing will have slightly different ideas on what the proper objective of fishery management should be. This has been neatly illustrated by David Cushing, who points out that the perfect management scheme for the individual fisherman is 'sink every other boat but mine'. This will give him both good catches and high prices for whatever he catches. No management scheme seems to have gone quite so far as this, though many are weighted in favour of the existing fishermen and their individual interests.

A common way of doing this is the prohibition of new methods of fishing, usually on the grounds (with or without scientific evidence) that they are damaging to the stocks. Not infrequently this means only that the established fishermen object to the new techniques, either because they are being driven out of business, or because they have to go to the expense of buying new equipment, and the trouble of learning how to use it. Such regulations have a long history, dating from the complaints of the use of trawls along the English east coast during the reign of Edward III in 1376.

Another ancient objective in controlling fisheries has been to maintain a supply of ships and men immediately available for the next war. The second world war was probably the last time the fishing fleets of an advanced country could be readily and quickly switched to naval purposes. In 1939 the larger British trawlers (several of which were German-built) were easily converted for antisubmarine patrols, while the smaller and older ships were admirable for minesweeping—not altogether surprisingly since many had been built for the purpose at the time of the first world war. Now both fishing and fighting has become too technically complex. Though the average modern trawler has more electronic equipment than a battleship of a few decades ago, it is not the most suitable for locating submarines or mines. Although this reason for maintaining or enlarging an active fishing fleet no longer holds good, the results of similar considerations may still be found in legislation affecting fisheries, e.g., in the U.S.A. laws concerning the use of foreign-built vessels (though this legislation has roots also in other considerations).

Also there are often social or political pressures towards maintaining a large fishing fleet for its own sake, or at least maintaining a large number of fishermen. In most countries fishermen come from local close-knit communities and cannot readily turn towards other occupations; often, too, they have political influence out of proportion to their actual numbers. Management measures, or other changes such as the introduction of an efficient but labour-saving type of gear, which are likely to put fishermen out of work or force them to turn to other employment, are likely to be successfully opposed even when they could lead to a more efficient fishery.

A variety of other objectives can be put forward as the aim of fishery management. Various ways of improving the lot of the individual fisherman are possible. Some of these—regulations aimed particularly at his safety or that of the vessel—are strictly outside the consideration of this book. There may be interaction with management or regulation in the present sense, since some regulations, e.g. a limit on the size of boat as a control on the amount of fishing, may tend to lead to a type of ship which is less seaworthy than that which would have developed in the absence of regulation (e.g. Crutchfield and Pontecorvo, 1969).

Management can also be introduced for the benefit of those outside the fishery. Most of the theoretical studies by economists have stressed the great benefits that could be provided to society as a whole by more rational management. Such benefits in terms of greater net economic yield from the fishery could be passed on to society in many forms, e.g., cheaper fish, more fish through the cross-subsidization of the development of new fisheries (it may be a condition of the granting of a licence to participate in an established, profitable, fishery that the licence holder also does some fishing in a new, developing, or currently less profitable fishery), or even a direct contribution to the national exchequer through substantial licence fees.

The introduction of regulations for the benefit of the public at large is, in fact, a rare event. Administrators in charge of the introduction and carrying out of measures of fisheries management are no more fond of extra work than other people. Most measures therefore come into existence as a result of specific pressures. A member of the general public is unlikely to press very hard for some fishery action which can at best benefit him to only a very small and often ill-defined extent. Fishermen on the other hand can and do protest very hard against the same measures if they think, rightly or wrongly, that they might seriously affect their livelihood.

A recent trend which favours paying more attention to the contribution to the national good as the major objective of management has been the increase of national planning. Typically, at least in western countries, fisheries management has been conducted as a contest, with the fishermen on one side trying to catch all and every fish they can, and on the other the manager bent on stopping him. This is obviously inappropriate where the management agency is also responsible for the planning and supervision of the fishing operations. This situation clearly occurs in the U.S.S.R. and other countries where fishing is a state-run business, but nearly all governments are now, to an increasing extent, becoming involved in the operational side of fishing—through such matters as granting of loans, subsidies, etc. These governments will have a considerable interest in any form of management which promises the opportunity to reduce such loans and subsidies.

Though the balance between objectives changes, at any time there will be a choice between different objectives open to one country, and the appropriate choice of objectives for that country is likely to be different from the choices for other countries fishing the same stock, or stocks, of fish. This choice of objective, which can easily develop into a more open conflict, has lead to the search for objectives of a fairly readily definable nature, which can be agreed upon as the general goal and against which any proposed regulation can be measured.

The most widely used objective of this kind is the maximum sustainable yield (MSY), i.e., the greatest physical yield that the stock can produce year after year. Nearly always the MSY has been defined in terms of the yield from a particular stock. It has been developed particularly from those biological curves of yield against fishing effort in which there is a pronounced maximum, especially the parabola derived from the simple Schaefer model.

The MSY has some obvious apparent advantages. The first is that it is based on a simple and easily understood picture of how a fish stock reacts to fishing. Any fisherman can understand that too small a stock will give a small yield, and also, with a little explanation, that only a small yield can be taken from a big stock without decreasing it. The other major advantage is that it is determined by a simple physical measure—the weight of fish caught—and is therefore independent of differences within or between countries on the relative values to be placed on catching more fish (or different kinds of fish) compared with savings in the costs of operations.

These advantages are, however, largely illusory. Stocks of fish do not behave in quite such a simple way, nor is it always at all easy to determine, if the stock does behave properly, precisely where the MSY occurs. Thus when there is a special need to have an agreed aim of management, from which a clear target, e.g., the catch to be taken in the forthcoming season, can be objectively determined, then it may be difficult to determine just what is the MSY, and the stock abundance required to achieve it. In this situation the concept of the MSY does not help in reaching a decision on management.

While the concept of the MSY has been criticized by biologists, e.g. Gulland (1968a, b), and indeed under the eumetric theory of fishing proposed by Beverton and Holt (1957), in which the size of first capture is always adjusted to the amount of fishing, there is no maximum in the yield curve, the strongest arguments against the concept have come from economists (e.g., Crutchfield and Zellner, 1963; Christy and Scott, 1965; Crutchfield and Ponte-corvo, 1969). They have pointed out that the attainment of the maximum physical yield makes no economic sense. Near the maximum the yield increases very slowly with increases in effort. In terms of the additional effort required to get it, the last ton of fish costs many times the average cost per ton. The costs of the effort exerted to take this last few fish would be very much better used elsewhere in the economy. Indeed, pursuing the MSY from an individual stock will, as pointed out by Gulland (1968a), reduce the total yield of fish from the sea compared with what could be obtained from the same total fishing effort, with a better balance between heavily fished stocks and less heavily fished ones.

Few would now defend the MSY as an abstract concept providing the ideal theoretical guide to management objectives. The theoretical arguments are now concerned with defining some level to the left of the point of MSY (if it exists) on the yield curve. However, in practice the concept can still be useful. Despite the volume of studies, many fish stocks continued to be overfished, and arguments continue over the desirability of doing anything to reduce the amount of fishing. In a not insignificant number of occasions it can be shown that the fishing effort has exceeded the level giving the maximum sustained yield. It is then a reasonably easy task to get agreement to cut the effort down to the level of the MSY—among the public at large there is enough growing awareness of the simpler aspects of fishery problems for the idea of exceeding the MSY to have achieved the moral stigma of a specialized form of pollution.

The reduction of fishing to the MSY level may not be as great a reduction as might be desirable, and there will remain waste of resources of money, ships, or men that might be more productively used elsewhere. However, a movement will have been made in the right direction. All those concerned in the fishery and its management will have become more familiar with the nature of the problems, of the difficulties that can arise, and of the benefits that might be obtained. This will make it easier to take further steps, based on more than the simplistic view represented by the concept of the maximum sustainable yield.

Theoretical studies (e.g., by Christy and Scott) have suggested the substitution of the maximum physical yield by the maximum net economic yield, or maximum rent. As discussed later, the net economic yield, e.g., the difference between the value of the catch and the cost of catching it, tends, in the long term, to become zero in an unmanaged fishery, may be quite small when fishing is at the level of the maximum sustained yield, and will have its maximum at a level of fishing somewhat less than that giving the greatest physical yield. The number of people having a direct interest in maximizing rent as such may be scarcely more than the number anxious to maximize physical yield—in fact without further explanation the general public may be more willing to support catching more fish, than attaining some abstract economic good. However, a high rent gives a better opportunity for satisfying several of the more immediate demands— better income for the fishermen, cheaper fish, or more revenue for the government (or at least a reduction in the need for subsidies).

This is the basic justification for choosing rent, or net economic yield, as the quantity that should be maximized for optimum management. There are other advantages. Expressing the objective in economic terms provides an immediate scale on which multi-species fisheries can be measured, and by which the competing needs of herring fishermen—who want lots of herring and no dogfish—and dogfish fishermen can, in principle, be resolved. Some other biological difficulties may be reduced. The curve of physical yield may be quite flat, with the maximum, if any, occurring at a high level of effort—often a level beyond that for which there are good data. The curve of net economic yield, on the other hand, is more sharply curved, with the maximum being more pronounced, and occurring at a lower level of effort, for which the information is better. Given the necessary economic information, it is easier for the scientists to determine, to a desired degree of precision, the value of the fishery mortality giving the maximum net economic yield, than to arrive at a value that will give maximum physical yield.

The great disadvantage of using net economic yield as an objective is that it depends on the price of the fish caught, and the unit costs of fishing. These will vary from year to year, and also from country to country. The net economic yield therefore does not provide a permanently fixed point for determining management action. Christy and Scott (1965) have pointed out that in the economist's perfect world, with free interchange between countries, the problems raised by national differences would disappear. In this, as in so many things, this world is not perfect; there is not a free flow of capital between, for example, U.S.A. and U.S.S.R., but in many areas fishing vessels from these two countries are exploiting the same stocks of fish, and many of these stocks are in need of management.

The position of the maximum net economic yield, as measured in terms of U.S.A. costs and values, will probably be different from that determined using Russian values. If management action depended on agreeing the exact objective, this would raise major difficulties. The important decision is, however, normally to decide on taking action, and on the general direction which should be taken. For this the different positions of the optimum on the basis of American or Russian economic factors may not be important—both will suggest a fishing rate rather below that giving the maximum physical yield, and often well below the present level.

The concept of the maximum net economic yield is therefore likely to promote movement in the right direction. It also stimulates deeper thought into the various non-biological factors at issue in managing any fishery. As progress is made towards the area in which various optima occur it is likely that the discussions and negotiations will become more complex and sophisticated. There will be less need for some simple formula to determine the action that shall be taken.

It may be noted that whatever the shortcomings of the maximum sustained yield as an objective of management policy, it has been popular in the past among those drawing up the preambles of fishery conventions. Thus, the Convention signed in 1949 setting up the International Commission for the North-west Atlantic Fisheries (I.C.N.A.F.) states in its preamble that 'The Governments . . . have resolved to conclude a convention . . . in order to make possible the maintenance of a maximum sustained catch from those fisheries'. Similarly the preamble to the Convention setting up the International Commission for the Conservation of Atlantic Tunas (I.C.C.A.T.) states that 'The Governments . . . desiring to cooperate in maintaining the populations of these fishes [tuna and tuna-like fishes] at levels which will permit the maximum sustainable catch . . .'.

The tuna Convention was signed in 1966. By 1969, when the Convention on the conservation of the living resources of the South-east Atlantic was signed, the criticisms of the MSY approach had taken effect, and the preamble to this Convention states no more than that 'The Governments . . . desiring to cooperate in the conservation and rational exploitation of these resources . . .', which does not commit the new Commission to any explicit object. More significantly, I.C.N.A.F. has been finding that the MSY objective may be restricting, and at its 1969 annual meeting passed a resolution which when it has been ratified will amend Article VIII of its Convention. This article is the main operative part of the convention and deals with the way in which the Commission, on the basis of advice from its Panels, recommends specific management actions to member governments. The proposed amendment replaces the basis of action from 'designed to keep the stocks . . . at a level permitting the maximum sustained catch . . .', to 'designed to achieve the optimum utilization of the

stocks . . . of fish . . .'. This, like the preamble to the South-east
Atlantic Convention, is non-committal, and allows plenty of
flexibility in choosing regulations which are in accordance both
with best current theoretical thinking, and with the immediate
needs of the fishery concerned (assuming such can be found). For
the present, I.C.N.A.F., like I.C.C.A.T., is formally bound to the
concept of a maximum sustained catch, with the limitation this
implies.

A major objection to the definitions of optimum management
strategy, and the arguments about which is the best—whether
maximum physical yield, maximum net economic yield, or some
other maximum—is that these distract attention from what is
often the real question, which is whether management action
should be taken at all. The comparison which always needs to be
made is between the results of any particular action, and of taking
no action. The results of taking no action have been described by
a number of authors (e.g., Gordon, 1954; Scott, 1955; 1962), and
can be readily summarized by reference to the relations between
total yield and amount of fishing derived in Chapter 4. In this
brief description there is no account of changes in the pattern of
fishing (sizes and ages of fish caught), since, although control of
the pattern is often an early aspect of management, e.g., by setting
minimum size limits for the fish that may be landed, such changes
affect the economic argument but little. The relations in Chapters
2 and 3 have been calculated in terms of weight of fish and
amount of fishing—strictly the fishing mortality. These need to
be converted in terms of money. While in most fisheries where the
fish is sold by auction the daily price of fish has a high negative
correlation with the amount landed, and there are similar relations
also over slightly longer periods, it is not so clear that the price of
fish landed from a particular stock varies much in the long term
(i.e., over periods of a year or longer) with the volume of landings
from that stock. To an increasing extent fish products are sold on
a world market—especially fish meal, shrimps, and tuna—or are
at least influenced by events in the world market. For instance,
the average price received by English trawlers for cod caught at
Iceland is determined, to a significant extent, in the long run by
the price of frozen fillets on the the Boston fish market—the
intermediate link being the volume of Norwegian frozen cod that is
sent either to America or England. So far as the catches from any
moderately small stock are concerned it is therefore reasonable to

treat the price as being independent of the quantity, i.e., the total value of the catch will be proportional to the weight caught.

Similarly it is reasonable to take the cost of fishing as proportional to the fishing effort, or fishing mortality. Most of the costs —fixed costs, labour costs, etc.—are determined by events in the national economy as a whole in which—with some exceptions, such as Peru and Iceland—fisheries are a very small element. In the long run therefore unit costs should be virtually independent of the amount of fishing.

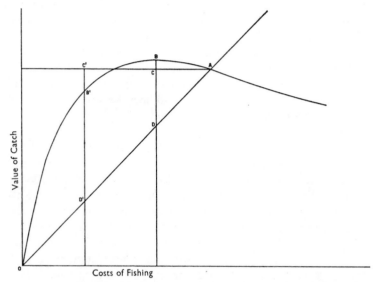

Fig. 20.—The relation between the value of the catch and the costs of fishing, showing the equilibrium position in the absence of controls (**A**), and the benefits from reducing fishing to the level giving the maximum gross yield (**B**), or the maximum net (economic yield) (**B′**).

The curves of yield against fishing effort can therefore, with appropriate change of scale, but no change in shape, be redrawn as curves of total value against total costs. A typical curve is shown in *Fig.* 20. Also shown in the figure is the line of equal costs and values, which cuts the yield curve at the point **A**. If the current position on the yield curve is to the left of **A**, it will be above the line, i.e., the value of the catch will exceed the costs. Assuming that the costs are taken to include a reasonable return on the capital invested, this implies that fishing will be a more than reasonably profitable operation. Further investment will be attracted, and the amount of fishing will move to the right. Conversely, if the effort happens to rise to a level beyond **A**, the value of the catch will be less than the total costs—i.e., the profit, if any, will be below the general level. There will be no attraction to enter the fishery and some incentive to leave, so that this effort will tend to decrease.

The point **A** therefore represents the point of equilibrium at which the fishery will arrive in due course, without the benefit of regulation, given a sufficiently long period of fairly steady costs and values. Conditions at this point can be compared with those at some other point to which the fishery might be guided by appropriate management actions. The first of these is the position of the maximum sustained yield, **B**. As drawn in *Fig*. 20, this is to the left of **A**, so that moving to this point will both increase the total value of the catch, and decrease the costs (for other forms of curve or for other cost–value ratios, **A** may be to the left of **B** and, according to some schools of thought, there would be no need to consider management).

The total benefit from moving to **B**, in terms of increased net economic returns, is equal to **BD** in *Fig*. 20 and made up of two parts; the increased yield (**BC**) and decreased costs (**AC**, which is equal to **CD**). As drawn, the latter is noticeably the larger. This is not necessarily so; the ratio of the benefits will depend on the precise shape of the curve—if it has a pronounced maximum there will be more likelihood of increasing the catch—and the costs and values, but the reduction in costs will always be an appreciable part of the possible benefits of moving from the long-term equilibrium to the point of maximum sustained yield.

These possible benefits will be greater from even further reductions in the amount of fishing. The maximum economic return (value less costs) will occur at the point **B'**, where the tangent to the curve is parallel to the line of equal costs and value (**OA**). The net economic return will be equal to **B'D'**. Compared with the zero return at the equilibrium point **A**, this return is made up of substantially reduced costs, **C'D'**, less a decrease in total catch **B'C'**. In this example, the catch, at the economic optimum, will be less than that at the unregulated equilibrium and also (as it must be) than the maximum sustainable yield. This is not universal; the catch at the optimum may be greater than the unregulated catch. What is universal is that a very great part of the possible benefit is the reduction in costs.

Another way of looking at the likely economic outcome of exploiting a stock of fish is in terms of the marginal yield (Gulland, 1968b). This may be defined as the increment in total yield achieved by adding one unit of fishing effort. It is therefore the

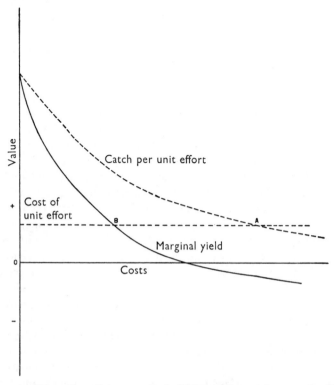

Fig. 21.—The value of the marginal yield, and the catch per unit effort, as functions of the total costs of fishing (fishing effort).

slope of the yield curves of Chapter 4, or, in economic units, of the curve in *Fig.* 20. This is shown as the full line in *Fig.* 21. The marginal yield starts at a high value and decreases continuously, cutting the *x*-axis at the point corresponding to the maximum sustainable yield. Naturally, any increase in fishing effort beyond this point will reduce the yield, so that the marginal yield is negative.

If the exploitation of a fish stock is carried out by a single enterprise, or the stock is under single ownership, then the marginal yield would be the main object of interest in determining whether or not to add to the current fishing effort, for example, whether to build a new vessel. If the value of the marginal yield is greater than the cost of a unit of effort, then the addition of the extra effort will be worthwhile—strictly additional investment in the fishery will be economically desirable if the value of marginal yield in the fishery is greater than the value of the additional production which would be obtained by investing the resources needed for the extra fishing effort in some alternative activity—fishing on another stock, or outside fishing altogether. That is additional fishing is justifiable if the line of marginal yield is above the level of the return from alternative employment, i.e., the horizontal line **AB** in *Fig.* 21. The long-term equilibrium position under single ownership will therefore be the point **B** where the line cuts the curve. It is of course approximately the same level of effort as that giving the maximum net economic return, **B'**, in *Fig.* 20.

Few fish stocks are under single ownership or are exploited by a single enterprise. The deciding factor in determining whether a company builds a new trawler, or whether a fisherman owning his own boat replaces it by a newer and more powerful one, is not the net addition to the total yield but the catches by the additional vessel. These will always be greater than the marginal yield (as defined above) to the extent that the additional effort reduces the stock abundance and hence the catches of the other vessels already fishing. The determinant of whether additional investment is made or not, is whether the curve of catch per unit effort (the broken-line curve in *Fig.* 21) is above or below the line **AB** giving the return from alternative investments. The long-term equilibrium point is where they intersect, at **A**, corresponding to the point **A** of *Fig.* 20. This is bound to occur at a higher, and often very much higher, level of effort then the equilibrium which would be reached under single ownership. The costs of the excess effort, plus a possible increase in catch, are the potential rewards of instituting management into an unregulated fishery.

While the preceding analysis does not predict a bright future for any fishery, it also does not predict a particularly black one, unless the yield-effort curve falls off sharply to the right of the maximum so that the catch under equilibrium conditions is very much less than the maximum possible. Although the catch is not worth more than the costs of capture (as it could be under ideal management), it should be at least equal to the costs. It has therefore been argued that the economics of the situation will make all fisheries self-regulating, and that even in the absence of management effort will be reduced if it reaches an excessive level. Apart from the fact that those putting forward this argument seem prepared to forego the considerable benefits that could be achieved, the actual losses in the absence of regulation may be much greater than the equilibrium analysis suggests.

In both the fish stocks and the fishery itself there are considerable lags. The abundance of the stock and the catch rates depend on the amount of fishing in previous years as well as on the current fishing. The level of fishing will be related to building plans for new vessels, and corresponding shore facilities, made some years previously, which in turn will probably have been determined on the analysis of fishing results even earlier.

At first these time-lags act for the benefit of the fisherman. The stock is more abundant than might be expected from the level of effort, and fishing can be very profitable. Indeed it is not uncommon in the early years of a new fishery, or after the introduction of a new technique, for the capital costs of a new boat to be paid off in a couple of years. As the effort approaches what would be the long-term equilibrium level these lags can be disastrous, causing the equilibrium position to be overshot to a great extent. When the effort is already past the equilibrium point new vessels may still be being added to the fleet which had been ordered at a time when catch rates were still high.

Once built, about all a fishing boat can do is fish. If the owner is fortunate the ship can be used in exploiting stocks other than those for which she was originally planned. Otherwise the decision on whether an existing ship is used or not is whether it is likely that the gross returns from the trip will exceed the running costs—fuel, equipment, and crew's wages. These costs will be much less than the total costs as defined earlier, and indicated by the lines in *Figs.* 20 and 21, which include all costs, including depreciation and a reasonable return on the capital employed. Some costs, such as insurance and major maintenance or repairs, may not be taken into account when deciding on the next trip, but will be when deciding to use the ship the next season or to lay her up.

If there are no alternative stocks, the only reductions in effort, even when it is beyond the long-term equilibrium, will be losses at sea and the laying-up or scrapping of those vessels which fail to cover even their running costs (including insurance and annual refit). An interim equilibrium may therefore be reached where the value of the catch equals these, smaller, costs, as shown by the broken line in *Fig.* 22—the total costs are again shown by the unbroken line.

This interim equilibrium, in which there is only enough money being earned by the fishery to cover the bare running costs, can

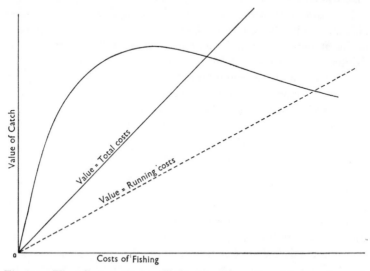

Fig. 22.—The effect on the equilibrium position when only running costs are considered.

last a long time. The classic example is the North Sea trawl fishery. Large numbers of trawlers were built in the first two decades of the century, some in the relatively good years right at the beginning of the century, and even more during the war (originally as minesweepers or patrol vessels) and just after—when for a couple of years catches were very good following the protection given to the stocks during the war. As a result the English fleet of trawlers suitable for fishing in the North Sea, but on few other places, mostly in the range of 90–120 ft., was by 1920 vastly in excess of the numbers that would be required for harvesting at the optimum rate, i.e., around the level of maximum net economic yield, and of the numbers that would be arrived at as the long-term equilibrium. Unfortunately, at least in this respect, the type of vessel concerned, with its simple and reliable steam engine, needed little upkeep, and if not immortal, was very long-lived—though by 1950 it was considered advisable to tread warily on the deck because the rust was only being kept together by the accumulated layers of paint. Although only 3 new trawlers were built in England specially for North Sea trawling between 1922 and 1950, the fleet in 1950, though old and inefficient, was still too large.

Economic forces alone cannot ensure that the level of fishing effort is adjusted downwards automatically from excessively high levels in a reasonably short time. Without going to the other extreme, and suggesting that without management all will necessarily be disaster, it is clear that even when no great loss of total catch is threatened (the North Sea trawl catch remained reasonably high throughout the inter-war period), some management action is often needed to prevent economic distress.

Another conclusion emerges from the North Sea story. Since the effect of wrong decisions—in the North Sea the decision to build more trawlers even in 1919/20—can last thirty years, it it would be highly desirable to avoid making these mistakes, rather than to attempt to put them right after they have been made. Once fishing has developed to too high a level of effort it can be a painful business to reduce it again, involving not only the premature scrapping of vessels with still a potentially useful life ahead of them, but also the resettlement of excess fishermen in other occupations. This may not be easy, even when they are comparative newcomers to fishing. For instance, most of the crews of the Peruvian anchoveta fishery, which developed within a decade from nearly nothing to annual catches of 10 million tons came from the mountainous interior of Peru. If they left fishing they would not go back inland, but join the thousands of underemployed squatters in the outer slums of Lima.

The best management should therefore be aimed at the prevention of excess effort, rather than be concerned only with the restoration of the situation after too heavy fishing has occurred. Management (in the sense used here) is not something that needs consideration only in the later stages of a fishery, after it has been developed. Rather, the problems of development and management need to be treated together. Thus, the Indo-Pacific Fisheries Council, at its 14th Session in Bangkok in 1970 emphasized that:

'The current concept of management encompasses a broader view taking into account several pertinent factors including social and economic factors. . . . Management in this sense is part of a comprehensive plan of development of a fishery, and should be considered in even the earliest stages of a fishery.' (I.P.F.C., 1971.)

So far in this discussion only the possible economic benefits of regulation have been considered. Equally important to the choice of management (including possibly having no management regulations) is the possible economic harm done. Since virtually all regulations are concerned with preventing fishermen doing something that they would otherwise want to do, the immediate economic effect is harmful—the fishermen affected will catch less immediately after the regulations are introduced than they would otherwise have done. Two things will reduce this damage: first, the regulations may also allow them to reduce the costs as well as their catch; secondly, the regulations should tend to increase the stocks, and in due time therefore restore the catches to the original level or better.

In the past the analyses of proposed regulations have been concerned mainly with the second of the effects. So long as the major objective was the maintenance of a high yield—if possible the achievement of the maximum sustainable yield—it was not entirely unreasonably to ignore the effects of regulation on the costs of fishing. The previous discussions have shown that the possible benefits from reducing costs are often as great as, and sometimes much greater than, the benefits from increasing total yield. Only if the yield-effort curve has a very sharp maximum— whale stocks are an obvious example—will most of the benefit come from increased yield alone. Ironically the International Whaling Commission—or more strictly its member countries, in discussions which took place outside the formal framework of the I.W.C.—during the negotiations on the allocation of quotas for Antarctic whaling to individual countries, was the first international fishery body to give due attention to the impact of its regulations on the cost of fishing.

The neglect of the effect on costs can be serious. Directly or indirectly most regulations concerned with limiting the amount of fishing will, in the long run, if not immediately, add to the inefficiency of the fishery, and prevent costs being reduced as much as they could be. This is most obvious in the earliest and simplest control, which is to ban the new and more efficient types of gear, but such methods as catch quotas, without other restrictions, will lead to progressive inefficiency. The economic effect of the regulations on the halibut fishery of the North-east Pacific has been well documented by Crutchfield and Zellner (1963). While very successful within its specified but restricted objectives of maintaining the stocks at a level giving high sustained physical yield, the regulations, through the various side-effects of the very short open season, did not allow the fishery to produce any appreciable net economic contribution to the North American economy—though this could have been a large proportion of the total gross value of the catch.

The economic effects, and particularly the long-term incidental effects, are also very important when considering the exploitation of more than one fish stock. While actual management measures have to be considered for each stock separately, measures on one stock can affect the success of fisheries on other stocks. The choice of regulations of one stock should take into account these possible interactions. Several types of interaction between the fisheries on the different stocks are possible. The simplest is when different stocks are exploited by the same fishery. A dozen species —principally cod, haddock, whiting, plaice, and sole—are caught in the North Sea trawl fisheries. Though each species has a slightly different distribution a single trawl haul in a suitable spot could catch individuals of all five major species. This fishery has been discussed in detail by Beverton and Holt (1957), who calculated curves of yield against fishing effort and against mesh size for several of the major species. They showed that the detailed shape of these was different for each species. It is therefore impossible (except maybe with very detailed and impracticable control of where each vessel fishes in the North Sea, thus maintaining the desired balance between catches of different species) to harvest all species at the optimum level (in whatever way the optimum might be defined). For instance, a mesh size large enough to let small cod escape, and thus grow and contribute to a larger cod catch later, would also allow all the well-grown soles or whiting to escape and result in a low catch of these species.

Beverton and Holt also calculated the combined yields of cod, haddock, and plaice as functions of fishing effort and mesh size, and optimization of this combined yield was suggested as a possible objective of management. Since plaice and cod—and still more sole and cod—fetch very different prices, combining them only makes sense if the total is expressed in economic terms, rather than gross weight. In terms of value, though, the combined yield curve could provide an adequate guide in choosing the objective of management of the stocks.

Not often are two or more stocks of fish as well mixed as the North Sea bottom fish—in fact it is an over-simplification to assume that they are so well mixed that the different species cannot be exploited to some extent independently. More usually a particular fisherman or group of fishermen will be interested primarily in one particular stock, or a small group of two or three stocks, but their catches will also include fish from other stocks which are the primary concern of other groups of fishermen. Thus the catches from any one of these latter stocks will be made up of a major part taken by fishermen fishing specifically for that species, and a lesser part taken by fishermen who are mainly interested in some quite different stock. The majority of haddock in the North Sea are taken by bottom trawls and other gear used by fishermen intent on catching primarily haddock, or at least a mixture of bottom fish among which haddock would be expected to be an important part. Some haddock are, however, caught by fishermen interested in quite different fish, including those trawling for herring. These latter catches include a high proportion of small haddock, since catching herring requires a small size of mesh, which retains the small haddock which would be released by the mesh sizes normally used in haddock fishing.

If the regulations and management of the North Sea were carried out with an objective determined solely in terms of haddock and the haddock fishery, then trawling for herring would need to be stopped, which would be impracticable. In this case, and in many similar situations the conflict in objectives between optimizing conditions for the haddock fishermen and not interfering with the herring fishery has been resolved in favour of the latter, or more specifically along the line of least resistance, which involves least interference with existing fisheries. That is, herring trawling with small meshes can continue, though with some check on the quantity of haddock caught.

Again, in a similar situation, the International Commission for the North-west Atlantic Fisheries (I.C.N.A.F.) in passing recommendations on the prohibition of the use in sub-area 4 off Nova Scotia of small meshes (under 114 mm. stretched mesh) for cod, haddock, and flounders (the mesh size itself being a compromise of different optimum sizes for different species), recommended that:

'In order to avoid impairment of fisheries conducted primarily for other species, and which take small quantitities of cod, haddock, and flounder incidentally, the Contracting Governments [shall] permit persons under their jurisdiction to take cod, haddock, and flounders with nets having a mesh size less than that proposed . . . so long as such persons do not have in possession on board a vessel fishing primarily for other species, cod, haddock, or flounders in amounts in excess of 5000 lb. or 2268 kg. for each or 10 per cent by weight for each, of all fish on board . . .'.

Conflicts in objectives between fisheries on different stocks have therefore been resolved either by considering the stocks concerned to be sufficiently mixed, and exploited as a single unit, so that they can be treated as a whole and a single objective determined, or, on the other hand, by treating the fisheries to be sufficiently distinct, and the interaction small enough, for the conflict to be ignored. Management therefore remains on a single stock basis, and there has not been any very general attempt to approach management of several stocks simultaneously.

A comprehensive approach may become necessary if the biological or operational interactions rise above a marginal level; for instance, if it proves impossible to operate a successful herring fishery without taking more than 10 per cent haddock. In that case the choice of objective—good haddock fishing or good herring fishing, or some combination—must be made. Either of the former choices will need, if it is to be accepted by everyone, some degree of compensation between the fishery whose interests are considered paramount, and the other whose activities will be in some way restricted in the former's interest. A combined objective will also raise considerable difficulties, though these are more of a technical nature rather than questions of principle. The scientists will have to solve tricky problems of determining the interaction in quantitative terms—just how much will the catches on both fisheries be affected immediately and in the long run by any particular measure that may be proposed. The economist will have to determine suitable functions to calculate the value of the joint yield (unless the price of the species is nearly equal, the combined yield in weight is not very meaningful), as well as of questions optimizing the net economic yield.

Though interactions in which the activities of one fishery can affect incidentally the stock principally exploited by another fishery are important, the type of interaction that is of greatest importance in determining the breadth of concern in fixing objectives, and choosing management measures, is the possible movements of ships between stocks of fish. Any successful management scheme, applied to a single stock, will result in resources of men and capital which might have been used in that fishery becoming available for use elsewhere. Possibly they are not used for fishing at all—and this possibility is greatest if, as suggested earlier, management is used to prevent surplus effort entering a fishery, rather than attempting to divert it once it has arrived—and then no further fishery problem arises.

More often the surplus effort will be diverted to some similar fishery. If the effort in this fishery is not too high, all will be well, and the diverted effort will add more to the overall total catch than if it had remained in the regulated fishery. Presumably though the actual return to the boats concerned will be less, otherwise they would have moved without pressure. However, their movement will increase the catches of the vessels remaining in the regulated fishery more than it will decrease the catches of those already in the second fishery. Because of this, as pointed out by Gulland (1968a), attempting to harvest the maximum physical sustainable yield from an individual stock, rather than the maximum net economic yield, or something close to it, will tend to decrease the total yield of fish from the sea.

More seriously, the alternative stock may itself be heavily fished. Then the diverted effort will not add, or add very little, to the total catch from that stock, but will of course add to the costs. Any improvement in the regulated fishery will therefore be offset by a worsening in the other fishery. It is not impossible, depending on the shape of the yield curves of the two stocks and the current position of the fisheries on them, for the regulation in fact to harm the overall position of the combined fisheries.

In such a situation the choice of objective of management is not difficult. Clearly it must be to improve the fisheries as a whole, rather than one fishery at the expense of another. The problems arise at the level of implementation. The interactions may require a view of fishery management problems which is wider either than that provided by the scientific advice—usually given on a basis of individual stock—or than the authority of the regulatory body immediately responsible. For example, urgently needed agreement on some reduction on the amount of fishing on the North Atlantic cod stocks has in part been delayed by this question of interaction. On the one hand two quite separate bodies, I.C.N.A.F. and N.E.A.F.C., are responsible for making recommendations on the west and east sides of the Atlantic respectively —and within the areas of competence generally initiate action on a basis of smaller sub-areas—while, on the other hand, many of the cod-fishing vessels, such as those from England, Germany, or U.S.S.R., can readily switch their activities from one side of the Atlantic to the other. There is therefore some feeling that the proposals being considered, e.g., for limitation of catch from the Arcto-Norwegian stock, cannot be of any long-term benefit to any except the local fishermen unless there is a simultaneous restriction for other stocks. This is of course not the only reason why agreement on reducing cod catches (and catches of other species) is proving difficult.

One last type of second-order effect of regulation should be mentioned—the long-range effect of regulations on the efficiency of the fishery. It has often been claimed by the apostles of free enterprise and of unrestricted fishing that the ultimate effect of restriction is to make the fishermen complacent and set in their ways, and to discourage innovation. On this argument the long-term effects will be to reduce the working efficiency of the fishery, and lose all the benefits in reduced costs that would theoretically come from proper management. Further, according to this school of thought, the lack of restrictions, and hence the dropping returns from the overexploited fishery, are the best kind of incentive for developing new fisheries in which the surplus effort can be better used. Against this it can equally well be argued that the uncertainties and losses involved in unrestricted fishing are so great, and may be becoming so notorious, that no sensible person would become involved in fishing. The feeling that there was no good long-term future in fishing, and the discouragement of the entry of new innovations or technical or managerial talent, could well lead to a similar decline in efficiency to that predicted as a result of regulation.

Most of these arguments are difficult to accept or reject as general propositions, and need to be discussed in relation to specific proposals. What they do imply, in relation to the present chapter, is that any regulation can have a number of surprising long-range effects, and that the viewpoint of those considering the introduction of management measures must be broad enough to take into account at least the more significant of these effects.

REFERENCES

BEVERTON, R. J. H., and HOLT, S. J. (1957), 'On the dynamics of exploited fish populations', *Fish. Invest., Lond.*, ser. 2, **19,** 533.

CHRISTY, F., and SCOTT, A. D. (1965), *The Commonwealth of Ocean Fisheries*. Baltimore: Johns Hopkins Press.

CRUTCHFIELD, J. A., and PONTECORVO, G. (1969), *The Pacific Salmon Fisheries. A Study of Irrational Conservation.* Baltimore: Johns Hopkins Press.

CRUTCHFIELD, J. A., and ZELLNER, A. (1963), 'Economic aspects of the Pacific Halibut fishery', *Fish. ind. Res.* **1**(1).

GORDON, H. S. (1954), 'The economic theory of a common property resource: the fishery', *J. Polit. Econ.*, **62,** 1924–42.

GULLAND, J. A. (1968a), 'The concept of the maximum sustainable yield and fishery management', *F.A.O. Fish. Tech. Pap.* (70).

GULLAND, J. A. (1968b), 'The concept of the marginal yield from exploited fish stocks', *J. Cons. int. Explor. Mer*, **32**(2), 256–261.

INDO-PACIFIC FISHERY COUNCIL (1971), 'The management of common use resources and the present situation in the I.P.F.C. area', *I.P.F.C. Proceedings 14th Session*, Sect. 2.

SCOTT, A. D. (1955), 'The fishery: the objectives of sole ownership', *J. Polit. Econ.*, **63,** 116–124.

SCOTT, A. D. (1962), 'The economics of regulating fisheries', in *The Economic Effects of Fishery Regulation* (ed. R. Hamlisch), *F.A.O. Fishery Reports* 5.

Chapter

6

THE TECHNIQUES OF MANAGEMENT

A REGULATORY body concerned with the management of a fish stock has available to it a variety of types of explicit regulations which can be introduced to achieve its purposes. Often a Commission or other body will include in its terms of reference a list of measures that it can consider. Sometimes this is merely a listing drawn up at the time of setting up the body, including all measures that delegates then thought might be useful, often with the catch-all item of 'other measures related to the objects of the Commission' at the end to encompass types of regulation that might have been forgotten. Other bodies have listings that explicitly, or by implication, exclude certain types that were thought, at least by some, to be objectionable. An example of this, in a fairly comprehensive list, is given by Article VIII (2) of the Convention on the conservation of the living resources of the South-east Atlantic, which reads:

'The matters with respect to which the Commission may make recommendations shall be:

(a) the regulation of the sizes of mesh of fishing nets;
(b) the regulation of the size limits of fish that may be retained on board any fishing craft or landed, or exposed or offered for sale;
(c) the establishment of open or closed seasons;
(d) the establishment of open or closed areas;
(e) the regulation of fishing gear and appliances, other than regulation of the size of the mesh of fishing nets;
(f) the improvement and the increase of living resources;
(g) the regulation of total catch by species, group of species, or, if appropriate, by regions; and
(h) any other type of measure directly related to the conservation of all fish and other living resources in the Convention

area [the waters of the South-east Atlantic from the River Congo southwards, and eastwards into the Indian Ocean as far as 40° E.].'

Though this is a fairly comprehensive list, two important items are not included—the direct control of the total amount of fishing, e.g., by a limit on the number of vessels, and the allocation of shares in any catch quota (or in any limited amount of effort) between countries. Allocation is discussed in a later section of the same Article, which suggests that any allocation should be arranged between the parties concerned, outside the framework of the Convention. This is the pattern already adopted in Antarctic whaling (*see* Chapter 2). It has the merit that the bargaining can be restricted to the players principally concerned, while the Commission as a whole decides only the somewhat less critical questions which do not impinge so directly on the activities of national fleets.

The possible regulations listed above and any other regulation can be placed in one or other of two groups (or possibly both) according to whether they affect the sizes or condition of fish caught (especially the minimum size) or the total amount of fishing. Their effect can then be determined, from one or other of the curves relating to the total yield to the amount of fishing, or to the size of first capture, as determined from the biological studies. If the regulation alters the sizes of fish caught in a more complex way than merely changing the size of first capture, the effect can be determined from such calculations as those in Chapter 4.

CONTROL OF THE COMPOSITION OF THE CATCH

Such regulations as a minimum landing size of fish or of the mesh size of trawl (or similar control of the type of gear, such as the size of hooks) clearly control the sizes of fish removed from the population. So will closed areas or seasons, provided there is sufficient difference in the sizes of fish caught according to season or area.

In principle such regulations change the costs of fishing little. A trawl with an 80-mm. mesh size in the codend will cost about the same as one of the same size with a 70-mm. mesh—probably in fact marginally less. It will also cost about the same to operate —again probably if anything slightly less since the large mesh will offer less resistance to being towed, and may also collect less rubbish which requires sorting out from the valuable catch by the crew.

There should therefore be no conflict in objectives in choosing the mesh size (or other regulation which controls the sizes of fish) which maximizes the physical yield. This will result in eumetric fishing, as defined by Beverton and Holt (1957).

Fisheries are rarely as simple as this. The regulations described will seldom if ever control the sizes of animals removed from the stock in such a neat fashion as suggested by the calculations of yield (or yield per recruit) as a function of size at first capture. This presumes that all animals below a certain size escape to grow to a better size, while all those above this size are liable to be caught at the full rate. The nearest approach to this occurs when there is a size limit and under-sized animals can be avoided, or if caught, returned to the sea alive and well. Thus whale gunners can fairly easily avoid whales appreciably below the size limit (and also whales with calves, whose capture is also banned). Traps will catch lobsters and crabs alive, and in most major lobster or crawfish (rock lobster) fisheries there is a strictly enforced size limit. There is some doubt, however, whether the under-sized lobsters, though they may be lively enough on the deck of the fishing boat, are in good enough condition to escape from predators, especially since they have been removed from their home ground and their well-known shelters. For this reason more attention has been paid in the important Western Australian rock lobster fishery (much the biggest Australian fishery in terms of value) to protecting the small animals by escape gaps in the traps (Bowen, 1963; 1971). These will allow the under-sized animals to escape, but retain the marketable ones.

Size limits for the landing of marketable fish are comparatively easy to enforce, since such enforcement takes place on shore, and often can be done at a limited number of major landing places. Such size limits therefore often form a convenient support to more effective measures for the protection of small fish—e.g., minimum mesh sizes, which are less easy to enforce.

The most widely used regulation to protect small fish, particularly in the great international trawl fisheries of the North Atlantic, has been the control of mesh size. The effects of using an enlarged mesh can be determined from the general models, but special methods have also been used. These can determine both the long-term effect, and also the effects in the interim period following the introduction of the large mesh, during which the losses due to the escape through the meshes of the small but still marketable fish, have not been made up by the increased catches of bigger fish—which are the survivors of the small fish that were allowed to escape (Gulland, 1961; 1964).

The escape of the small fish is, for the changes in mesh size generally considered, only a minor percentage of the total catch in weight, and less in value. When a big change in mesh size is considered, it will usually be introduced in stages at each of which the immediate loss during the interim period will be small. However, such losses can be a major obstacle to the easy acceptance by the fishermen of the larger mesh. He can often see some of the fish escape while the net is being hauled as it comes up beside the ship—and these fish in the water will often look larger than they really are. His losses can be directly observed, while the gains are more hypothetical, being in the future, and also dependent on the adoption of the larger mesh by all, or the majority of, those exploiting the same stock.

The objectives raised because of the escape of marketable fish are increased by the lack of sharpness in the selection by a trawl. For instance, the analysis may show that the release of cod in the Iceland fishery up to a size of 35 cm. is desirable. Further experiments can be made which show that this length corresponds to the 50 per cent selection length of a 110 mm. mesh. That is, of the fish of this length that enter the net, half will escape through the meshes and half will be retained. However, some fish as large as 40 cm. or more will escape while some fish as small as 30 cm. will be retained (c.f. *Fig.* 9). This also makes minimum landing sizes of fish less useful as an aid to the enforcement to mesh regulation. If the minimum size is set at 35 cm., fishermen fishing with a legal mesh will catch under-sized fish, and have to either risk prosecution or discard them at sea, which will be wasteful if, as generally happens, the chance of survival of the fish is small. Alternatively, a minimum size as low as, say, 30 cm., will still leave some incentive to use a mesh somewhat below the legal size.

The spread in selection varies with the kind of fish. Soles seem to be active and skilful at finding a mesh through which they can escape. Their selection is therefore fairly sharp, and regulation of mesh size gives a good control of the sizes of sole which are caught. On the other hand, shrimps and prawns can easily get entangled and though a large mesh size will select out the smaller shrimp the selection is very imprecise, and a lot of small shrimp will be retained by a mesh that is large enough to let some very large shrimp escape. Mesh regulation is therefore not often efficient as a management measure in a shrimp fishery. Often these fisheries catch large quantities of fish as well as shrimp, frequently small individuals of species that when full grown are of present or potential commercial value. Designs of trawls exist (High, Ellis, and Lusz, 1969) which allow most of these fish to escape, while retaining the shrimp. The important element in the design is a sloping wall of large mesh within the net. The fish can pass downward and through the mesh, and thence out, while the shrimp pass upward along and over the barrier and are retained. Though the use of such a gear would probably be difficult to enforce, often the shrimp fishermen are glad to use it because of the time saved in sorting the catch.

The mesh regulations in the North Atlantic have been based on careful scientific assessments both by individual scientists or laboratories (Beverton and Holt, 1957; Graham, 1954), and also by international working groups with members from all the main countries (*see* Beverton and Hodder, 1962, and also the annual reports made by the I.C.E.S. Liaison Committee and the I.C.N.A.F. Assessment sub-committee). Where these reports showed larger mesh sizes to be useful and practicable these have by now been generally adopted. However, the reports, and especially that by the I.C.E.S. working group, emphasized two major weaknesses of mesh regulation as the sole management measure—first, that most trawl fisheries operate on a mixture of species, and the optimum mesh sizes for different species may be very different; and secondly, that while mesh regulation can increase the total catch to some extent, the economic benefit will be short-lived unless there is some control of the amount of fishing. The greater the gain from mesh regulation (or any similar measure) the shorter time is the full benefit likely to last. As soon as the catches begin to increase, extra effort will be encouraged to enter, and this will tend to depress the catch per boat back to the original level—though the total catch will probably remain higher than before the regulation was introduced.

This latter shortcoming applies to all methods of controlling the type or size of fish caught, and not merely to mesh regulation. The other methods, such as the banning of fishing at times and places when small fish are abundant, are at best little more successful at increasing the effective size at first capture, and are equally ineffective in reducing the excess costs involved in exerting too high a fishing mortality. On theoretical grounds, indeed, there is, except in a few special circumstances, little if any justification for the introduction of closed areas or closed seasons. Despite this, such regulations continue to be put into force. They do have a number of advantages, particularly for a harassed administrator faced with a demand to take some action, but an unwillingness on the part of some or all of the fishermen to accept the theoretically more desirable types of regulation.

Closed areas, or closed seasons, have the major advantage that they are relatively easy to be enforced, and still more can be very easily seen to be enforced and observed. They are also very simple for the fishermen or others to understand, and are therefore often introduced, and cheerfully accepted, when their only effect is the purely psychological one of enabling the fishermen and administrators to have the satisfactory feeling that something is being done.

Both measures can be used to control either the amount of fishing or the sizes or kinds of fish caught. The former use is discussed in detail below. The second use is not always possible. Clearly if the composition of the catches is the same wherever or whenever fishing is done, no pattern of closed seasons or closed areas will change the composition of the total catch. Nearly always there will be some differences—for instance, the proportion of mature fish will increase near the time and place of spawning— and even in the tropics where some spawning may occur throughout the year there will usually be certain seasons when spawning is more intense than the year-around average.

Special protection of mature or spawning fish may well not be of any real conservational benefit. It is more certain that the protection of small fish, below some optimum size at first capture, will increase the long-term average catch. Such protection can be effected when small fish tend to congregate in particular nursery areas. For instance, the pattern of life of the North Sea plaice is for the baby fish, not long after they hatch, and immediately after they have taken the typical asymmetrical flatfish shape, to drift inshore to the very shallow water along the coast—particularly the Dutch and Danish coasts. As they grow they slowly move offshore. When they first reach a marketable size, at two to four years old, they are still relatively close inshore and in shallow water. The deeper waters, north of the Dogger Bank, are only inhabited by old large fish. Closing of the shallow nursery areas would therefore give protection to the young fish and allow them to grow. This benefit can be achieved even without regulation if some other factor encourages the diversion of fishing from nursery areas to those inhabited mainly by larger fish. Such a change occurred in the English plaice fishery around 1960, when more trawlers, especially the new and larger motor trawlers, concentrated their operations in the deeper waters north of the Dogger Bank. This led to a sharp rise in the average size of fish in the English catches, and a fall in the numbers of small fish. As could be expected, by allowing the small fish to grow to a good size, this resulted in an appreciable increase in the weight landed, even though the numbers caught actually decreased (Gulland, 1968).

The opportunity to protect small fish by closing certain nursery areas also occurs in other fisheries. For example, the Faxa Bay area of south-west Iceland is an important nursery area, not only for plaice, but also for haddock and, to a lesser extent, other species. This area was studied by an international group of scientists in the 1930s (Tåning, 1948), and they concluded that the closure of the inner part of Faxa Bay to trawling would be beneficial. Such a closure has been put into effect since then as part of Iceland's move to increase her control over the fish stocks and fisheries around her coasts. This included the so-called 'cod war' between Iceland and England, during which the British Navy was engaged in escorting British trawlers fishing in the zone within the extended limit lines. These waters within the twelve-mile limit, drawn across between headlands, were claimed by Iceland as being within national jurisdiction, but at that time were considered by England as being on the high seas. It is somewhat ironic that the English trawler fishermen have probably benefited as much as anyone by the closure of the coastal zone to trawling. Certainly they have suffered some inconvenience, and even danger, by being unable to fish in the coastal zone. However, there are still plenty of areas outside the twelve-mile limit where fishing is usually as good—the situation for the English fishery would be very different if the limits were extended to the edge of the continental shelf. The cod stocks, which are the major bottom fish in the Icelandic fishery, were not much affected by the limit change. The main effect was on haddock and plaice, for which significant nursery areas were closed to trawling, and these species are relatively more important in the English fishery than in the Icelandic fishery.

These examples, such as the plaice in the North Sea or around Iceland, are exceptions. Only in relatively few stocks is there such a nicely defined separation between large and small fish that the closure of nursery areas can be used as a reasonably exact control on the sizes of fish that are caught.

A slightly separate use of closed areas or seasons is for the protection of fish either when they are spawning, or when they are on the way to spawn. This is in principle a very worthy objective. It is the spawning fish which produce the young fish to support the future of the fishery. If not enough manage to spawn there will be few young fish and the fishery will collapse. This principle is a direct extension from the management of stocks of mammals such as deer, where the failure to maintain a good breeding population quickly leads to a decline in the stock.

There are, however, important differences between mammals and most marine fishes in respect of their reproductive capacity. Mammals produce few young—only one every other year in the case of the blue whale—and even in the most favourable conditions it is impossible for a small adult population to produce more than a moderate to small number of young. On the other hand many species of fish produce enormous numbers of eggs, a matter of several thousands in all but the least fecund animals, up to several millions in the case, for example, of a large cod. If all these survived it would not take many adults to produce reasonable numbers of young to maintain the future of the fishery. Of course, under average conditions very few do survive—if the population is stable, neither increasing nor decreasing, a mature female will produce, on the average, during her life, just two offspring that survive to maturity. However, it seems that if the adult population decreases, conditions for the young improve—there is less competition between each other, or between adults and young, for food and living space; also many adult fish are no respectors of the young of their own species, and treat them like any other small animal, as a suitable food—there is therefore better survival, and the actual number of young fish may not decrease much even when the adult stock is significantly reduced. Protection of the adult stock as such is thus not often a matter of high priority within the general pattern of managing the fishery. Even when it is important to maintain a good spawning stock this is not guaranteed by protecting only the spawning or pre-spawning fish. If the fishing on the immature fish is sufficiently intense, the abundance of a year-class of fish can be so reduced before it approaches maturity that there would not be enough adult fish even if there was no fishing on them. There are still some occasions when a closure of a spawning fishery may be desirable, or at least more desirable than any practicable alternative. Often the fish are concentrated at or just before the time of spawning, and are then very easily caught in large numbers. In a world managed in accordance with simple economic logic this would be the best time to fish. It would be the time whan a given catch could be taken at least cost, and often also when the catch would have its greatest value, since the pre-spawning fish are often in the best condition. However, because the fish are readily caught, any excess in the capacity of the fishing fleet can very soon lead to a serious reduction in the stock. Political considerations may make it difficult to apply the necessary restriction to the size of the fleet, and the best available method to ensure adequate protection of the stock is to stop fishing during the spawning season.

Similar considerations apply to other techniques to protect the spawning fish. The best known of these is probably the protection of so-called 'berried lobsters'. These are females carrying eggs, which after being laid are attached to the underside of the lobster until they hatch. In England the landing or sale of such berried lobsters is prohibited. Though there is a long tradition of the evasion of such laws by scrubbing the lobster to remove the eggs, the regulations are generally obeyed. So much so that most fishermen have the belief of the need for such regulations so well absorbed that it has been difficult to persuade them that probably the regulation is not needed. Most likely the additional number of larval lobsters produced would not make any difference to the number of young lobsters recruiting to the fishery some years later, or if it did, then an equally effective measure would be a reduction in the catches of smaller and less valuable females.

CONTROL OF THE TOTAL AMOUNT OF FISHING

The regulations discussed so far have been aimed at controlling the composition of the catch, especially the sizes of fish caught. The other and more important and fundamental objective is the control of the amount of fishing. This may be controlled more or less directly, by limits, say on the number of ships operating, or by limiting the total catch, or indirectly, such as by closed areas or seasons, or by regulation of the type of fishing gear that can be used.

The last can be dismissed fairly quickly. In this connexion the prohibition of a particular type of gear is only effective when that gear is especially efficient. It is usually proposed in order to protect the interests of an established group of fishermen at present using a less efficient gear, who are unwilling to go to the expense of buying new equipment, or to go to the trouble of learning to use it. It may happen, e.g., because of political pressures, that the desires of this group should receive priority in determining management policy. Such a deliberate action in reducing the efficiency of the fishery is clearly undesirable on a broader view of the objectives of management, especially because, as shown in Chapter 5, the largest potential benefit from many management measures is economic, and comes from the ability to reduce costs. Such reduction of costs will be small, if they exist at all, if the efficiency of the fishery is reduced by the management action.

Nevertheless such regulations of the type of gear that may be used are not uncommon. They are best justified where the biology of the fish is such that an increased fishing mortality can lead to an appreciable decrease in the total yield, and where there are constitutional or similar obstructions to limiting free entry to the fishery. Under these circumstances, if the most efficient gear is allowed to be used, it may be difficult to prevent the fishing mortality from rising too high—even with detailed restrictions on the extent of its use. A ban on using it will at least ensure that the catch is maintained at a high level. The obvious example is the salmon fisheries of the Pacific coast of North America.

Apart from some fishing, mainly by the Japanese, on the feeding grounds in the open Pacific, the salmon are harvested as they approach the rivers up which they go to spawn. By far the most effective way of catching these fish is by means of fixed traps at or near the mouths of the rivers; suitably located it can almost be arranged for the fish to swim straight into the processing plant. Catching costs are reduced to a minimum. Such traps are far too efficient and a well-placed trap can remove nearly all the fish arriving, leaving few to spawn, and therefore few fish to support the fishery in two to four years' time. This is indeed what happened soon after large-scale salmon fishing started on the American Pacific coast. Faced with declining stocks, and at that time no detailed scientific study on which more sophisticated management policies could be based, some immediate action was required if many of the salmon runs were to be preserved. The prohibition of the use of traps was both politically acceptable and also reasonably effective in preventing the collapse of the stock. As an emergency measure half a century or more ago, such efficiency-reducing regulation then made sense, even on a purely economic basis—better an inefficient fishery than no fishery at all. However, the history of North American salmon management since then has been, until recently, a matter of increasing complex measures to restrict the efficiency of the industry in order to limit its capacity to the potential of the resource. Economists have strongly criticized the result as an outstanding example of irrational conservation (e.g., Crutchfield and Pontecorvo, 1969). However, the measures have probably resulted in higher employment in areas such as Alaska, where alternative occupations are scarce. Also most measures to increase efficiency would require restriction of free entry to the fishery, and such restriction has generally been considered to be unconstitutional in the United States. In an age of increasing uniformity, dominated by the large and impersonal company, there is much to be said for the continued existence of the independent salmon fishermen, however inefficient they may be by strict economic accounting. It is, though, ironic that such independence is only assured by strict controls on the type of gear used and the times and places of fishing.

The salmon fisheries also provide good examples of control of the amount of fishing by means of closed areas and closed seasons. As the salmon return to their parent streams after feeding and growing in the open Pacific, they are exploited in the coastal waters of Canada and the United States. Following the great volume of research on these salmon stocks the number of fish returning in each stock can be reasonably well estimated—partly from data available before the fishing starts and more precisely from information coming from the fishery as it progresses. Estimates are also available on the optimum escapement, that is the optimum number of salmon that should be allowed to escape through the fishery and enter the rivers. Too few, and there are too few eggs to produce young salmon for the future; too many, and the fish will interfere with each other on the spawning beds—the latecomers will disturb the eggs deposited by the earlier spawners—leading possibly to a reduction in the number of young produced, and certainly involving a smaller current harvest than would be possible if these extra fish were caught before going upstream.

Subtracting this optimum escapement from the total numbers of salmon migrating in toward the parent rivers gives the number of fish that should be caught. Since, even though traps have been banned, the existing fleets of salmon vessels could in most areas catch this amount several times over in the period between the arrival of the salmon off the coast and their passage upstream, a complex system of regulations has been introduced. This system is adjusted to keep the total catch within the desired limits, while maintaining the balance between the different sectors of the industry. In the United Sates, excluding Alaska, sports fishermen take a substantial part of the harvest, especially of chinook and coho salmon, while different groups of commercial fishermen use gill nets, purse seines, and trolling gear. Each of these types of gear is only allowed to be used at certain times and places. The open areas are chosen to minimize physical interference between gears, to maintain a reasonable balance between different gears, and to ensure the correct catch of each species and from each of the separate stocks—the salmon from each river, and often from each part of the river form separate stocks, and should be managed separately. In addition, so far as the salmon from the Fraser River are concerned, the International Pacific Salmon Fisheries Commission has to adjust its regulations to ensure equal catches by U.S.A. and Canadian fishermen. This is no easy task when the fish are moving in succession through international waters and the coastal waters of the U.S.A. and Canada on their way to the Fraser River, toward the southern end of British Columbia. The fact that this equality is usually very closely achieved, as are the target figures for the escapement, is a tribute to the competence of the staff of the Commission. It also shows the precision of management that can be achieved, even in an international fishery, when the controlling agency has sufficient authority to introduce detailed regulations, and to modify them literally from day to day in the light of current information from the fishery—though it might be noted that much of the complicated admistrative, scientific, and enforcement procedure could be eliminated if shares in the available catch could be directly allocated to individual enterprises who could be allowed to harvest their allocation in the most efficient manner possible.

Closed areas and closed seasons, often in combination, have been used in many other fisheries to limit the amount of fishing (i.e., the fishing mortality) to the desired level. These methods have usually been chosen more for the comparative ease with which they can be explained to the fishermen and enforced, than for the effectiveness with which the ultimate objectives of management can be achieved. No involved inspection or control mechanism is needed—if fishing is being done in the closed areas or at the closed season then the regulations are being broken, and if all fishing is stopped for a given species even inspection at sea is not necessary. The fishermen can easily understand the basis of the rules—too much fishing is being done, and too many fish are being caught so some fishing must be stopped.

The trouble with this technique is that it offers little opportunity of reducing the costs of the fishery. By the nature of the regulation the overhead costs, including depreciation, will remain unaltered, except to the extent that they can be spread over fisheries on other stocks to which the vessels concerned can be diverted during the closed seasons. Immediately following the introduction of closed seasons (but not closed areas) there should be a reduction in running costs as the vessels are laid up, or used in other fisheries, though there is a limit to which some of the running costs, such as crews' wages, can be saved. Where the fishery concerned is an important local industry—or even, as in the case of the Peruvian anchovy, in the country as a whole—the loss of employment through the laying up of the fleet for a period can lead to social difficulties. More important, the closed season is usually, but not always, set when it will be most effective—that is, when catches are highest. At that time the cost of catching a given weight of fish, i.e., of exerting a unit amount of fishing mortality, will be lowest. Introducing the closed season will therefore increase the average cost of a unit amount of fishing mortality. Moreover, in the long run, if the regulations are successful in building up the fish stocks, additional catching capacity will be attracted into the fishery—new boats will be built and existing ones modernized or replaced. Unless the open season is shortened, or the closed areas extended, the fishing mortality will tend to return to its original level. There is therefore likely to be the need, once closed areas or seasons are introduced, for them to be continually extended to maintain the amount of fishing (fishing mortality) at the desired level. This effect is discussed in more detail below in connexion with catch quotas. Clearly a conservation measure that results in the ships being laid up for an increasing proportion of the year cannot be expected to lead to economic efficiency. Despite this, closed seasons or closed areas have been, and are likely to remain in the future, a common method of regulation, especially as an initial step. Often they are the control that is most readily accepted by fishermen; once introduced, and the problems observed in practice, it is less difficult to move on to other forms of regulations.

These regulations are some direct form of control in the amount of fishing. Such controls can be classified in two ways—by how the amount of fishing is measured, and how the operations of the individual fisherman are affected. Ultimately the amount of fishing must be measured by the scientist in terms of the fishing mortality, i.e., the proportion of the fish stock removed in a given period. This cannot be measured directly—even in the most favourable case, such as migrating salmon, the run is known with precision only at the end of the fishing season—and the two obvious measures that can be used are the weight caught, and the fishing effort, in terms of, for example, the number of days fishing by vessels of a standard type.

The regulatory authority may then set a limit to the catch of say 10,000 tons of fish, or to the effort at say 4000 standard days fishing. The choice then is of allowing all fishermen to operate freely until the quota is reached, and then all stop; or, of allowing only a limited number of fishermen to operate more or less freely and continuously. This gives four basic types of control, all with their own particular problems, and all potentially useful. In practice the most used has been the unallocated catch quota, while unallocated effort quotas have rarely if at all been used. On the other hand, where some form of licensing has been used as control, allowing only a few fishermen to operate freely, the licence has more often been in terms of the vessel, i.e., of effort, rather than of catch.

The disadvantage of using catch as a measure of fishing mortality is that the ratio of catch to mortality varies in accordance with changes in the abundance of the stock. Then if the stock fluctuates for reasons unconnected with the fishery the catch quota needs to be adjusted each season to maintain the mortality at the desired level. In many northern fish stocks, such as the haddock in the North Sea or the Arcto-Norwegian cod, the strength of a year-class (the number of young surviving from each year's spawning) varies greatly. In both 1962 and 1967 spawning conditions for haddock in the North Sea appear to have been exceptionally good so that in 1964–66 and again in 1969 and later (most haddock caught in the North Sea are between two and four years old) catches were very good. Catch quotas in those years would have had to have been increased, if they had been in operation, to keep the mortality at the desired level, and ensure that the exceptionally abundant production from these year-classes was not wasted. Conversely, year-classes in the Arcto-Norwegian cod seem to have been weak between 1965 and 1968. These cod make their major contribution to the trawl fishermen when between four and seven years old—though they do not enter the fisheries on the mature stock, carried on by a variety of gears, until about nine years old. Therefore any catch quota for the trawl fishery around 1972/73 would have to be set below the long-term average catch.

In these fisheries—North Sea haddock and Arctic cod—reasonably good estimates of the strength of the year-classes are available before they enter the fishery from surveys of young fish carried out by research trawlers. The Russians have carried out surveys of young cod for about twenty years. These surveys enable first estimates of the abundance of a year-class to be made during the first autumn of life. At this time the young cod, which are spawned in the early spring in the Lofoten Islands area of northern Norway, and then drift northward and eastward in the prevailing current, take to living on and close to the bottom where they can be sampled by trawls. Better estimates of year-class strength can be obtained in the next three years, before the fish recruit to the fishery, at about four years old. Changes in abundance due to changes in year-class strength can in this fishery therefore be estimated well in advance—though always subject to revision as better information from the fishery, and on the age composition of the catches, becomes available. Thus the catch quota can be adjusted to maintain the fishing mortality at the desired level, and the adjustments can to a large extent be made in advance of the season.

For some other fisheries it may be less easy to predict changes in stock abundance. Then, when an average quota is set in a year when fish are scarce, the fishing mortality may rise to an undesirably high level. At other times a strong year-class may enter the fishery but be under-utilized because the quota is not adjusted in time. Though such losses may be serious when they occur, they are only likely to be large when there is a combination of unfavourable circumstances: the fluctuations in abundance must be large; the fish must be short-lived—otherwise over- or under-exploitation in one year could be made up by suitable adjustments in the second year; and the estimation of strength of the young pre-recruit year-classes must be difficult or expensive. Otherwise the advantages of measuring the amount of fishing in terms of catch—such as easy comprehension by the fishermen and direct comparability between different fishermen—would favour the use of that measure.

On the other hand, determining the point when the desired value of fishing mortality has been reached by some measure of the amount of fishing or fishing effort—number of vessels, number of days at sea, etc.—does seem to have some advantages over using catch as a measure. If the measure of effort used is a good one, then it should be directly proportional to the fishing mortality, irrespective of any changes in the abundance of the fish stock. No problems of year-to-year adjustments to the quota to take account of year-class or other fluctuations need arise, nor will the difficulties of getting adequate measures of the strength of the recruiting year-classes.

However, it is not in practice easy to get a measure of fishing effort which will remain proportional to fishing mortality. Two major problems arise; one of detecting and measuring changes in efficiency, i.e., the ratio of nominal effort to fishing mortality caused, and the other of comparing and calibrating efforts by two or more distinct fleets. While methods have been developed for comparing the relative fishing effort, or more strictly fishing power, of different vessels, and these have been applied to a number of fisheries (e.g., Gulland, 1956; Robson, 1966), these are most suitable for comparing vessels of the same type, e.g., trawlers fishing at the same time or at least in the same season. It is less easy to compare completely different types of vessels, or, what is more serious from the point of view of management, to compare the fishing mortality caused by a nominal unit fishing effort exerted by the same fleet in successive years. Fishermen are always trying to increase their efficiency; sometimes this is only achieved by individuals learning better the tricks of the trade, and in this case it may be expected that the general improvement of those fishermen staying in the fishery will be balanced by the retirement of the oldest and the entry of new and unskilled men. Usually there are also technical advances, some of which are obvious, e.g., the building of larger and more powerful trawlers, the effect of which can be readily measured by comparing their catches with those of smaller and old ships. Other changes are more subtle, e.g., the use of better navigational equipment. Thus the efficiency of the Peruvian anchovy fleet was increased by the introduction of echo-sounders, power blocks for better handling of the net, and fish pumps for quickest extraction of the fish from the nets into the hold. Boerema, Saetersdal, and Valdivia (1965) estimated that these changes increased the efficiency, i.e., the resulting fishing mortality, of the unit of effort used (a trip to sea of a standard-sized vessel) by 20 per cent, but this was more a result of inspired guesswork than of mathematical calculation.

Such guesswork is quite acceptable in the context of attempting to obtain the best estimate (based on the catch per adjusted unit of effort) of the changes in the abundance of the fish stock. It would be much less acceptable if it were used to adjust the quotas received by one section of a fishery—a particular country or a group of vessels. For example, the cod stocks off West Greenland are exploited by a wide range of vessels—local small inshore boats, modern stern trawlers from Germany and other European countries, and dory vessels from Portugal (see Statistical Bulletins of I.C.N.A.F.). The last used methods that have not changed for centuries—fishermen going out from the mother ship (among which the old sailing schooners have not been entirely replaced by motor vessels) each in his own small boat to catch cod with hand-lines. Compared with their constant efficiency, that of the trawlers increases from year to year. Often these changes are not easy to quantify, e.g., when the technique of fishing the midwater schools of inactive post-spawning fish was developed. A guess might be made that this innovation would increase the effectiveness of a standard unit of trawl effort (e.g., an hour's fishing by a trawler of standard size) by 15 per cent, so that if the amount of fishing was measured in terms of effort the number of standard hours fishing would have to be reduced by 15 per cent. The Germans might well feel that this was too great, while the Portuguese that it was too small. The only objective test of the relative changes in efficiency of the two gears would be the changes in relative catch, which in effect means measuring the amount of fishing in terms of catch not effort.

Another difficulty in using fishing effort as a direct measure of fishing mortality is that many of the adjustments made by scientists to the most readily observable data depend on reports by fishermen which are almost impossible to verify. For example, fishing effort is usually calculated as the product of fishing power of the vessel and the fishing time. The only measure of fishing time of say a trawler that is readily observable and enforceable is the number of days at sea, whereas the real fishing time is the number of hours with the trawl actually fishing on the bottom. This is obtained by direct reports from the fishermen, and an obvious feature of the English distant-water fishery in the post-war period has been the increase in the number of hours fishing per trip (Gulland, 1956). Regulation of the number of days at sea would fail to take this into account, while regulation of the number of hours fishing would be impossible to enforce.

Precise regulation of the amount of fishing by control of the nominal fishing effort therefore raises serious obstacles. The chief use of such controls then probably occurs when no very precise management is desired, but rather some simple method of preventing serious deterioration of the situation is needed pending the introduction of a more sophisticated system. The simplest, and thus in some ways the best, measure is just the number of vessels, so that a limit is placed on the number of ships that can operate in a given fishery. This is generally only possible in a fishery under single national jurisdiction, or where one country accounts for the great bulk of the total catch, but can then be very effective. The highly successful development of Japanese fishing away from the home islands included as a very important element the restriction of the number of licences to engage in each fishery. The number of licences was set to ensure that each participant should get a good living, and when the resource was valuable, but limited, as in the North Pacific high seas salmon, the returns to those allowed to enter the fishery were extremely good. The existence of such successful fisheries, and the assurance that, at least so far as Japanese fishermen were concerned, any such success in a new fishery would not be threatened by a flood of new participants, were major factors in the expansion of Japanese fishing across the whole world.

Control of the number of ships has also been useful at the other extreme, where political difficulties make any enforcement or inspection, other than observation of the ships on the grounds, impracticable. In the East China Sea it has long been clear that the demersal stocks were too heavily fished. Because of the severe political difficulties in the area—the main fishing countries are Japan, China, Taiwan, and both North and South Korea—it is impossible to set up the kind of intergovernmental Commission that is becoming standard elsewhere in the world. With no formal machinery available for complicated multi-national agreements, nevertheless a number of bilateral arrangements have been made. Under these the amount of fishing has been limited, and this has been done in terms of the number of vessels. These include provisions under treaty between Japan and the Republic of Korea and also agreements made between China and the Japanese fishing industry (Shindo, 1971). In each case the number of trawlers from each side that can operate in a number of different areas during the main fishing seasons is specified.

ALLOCATION OF SHARES AND LIMITED ENTRY

Whether the amount of fishing is measured by catch or nominal fishing effort, there remains another critical decision as to how to ensure that the desired limit is not exceeded. In simple terms two solutions are possible—either to allow free fishing by anyone until the desired level has been reached (the simple quota system) or to allow only the limited number of fishermen required to cause the desired mortality but allowing them to fish freely (the limited entry system). Naturally enough, intermediate systems occur in actual practice, but the essential distinction is between a single open quota and a limited entry.

The single quota has often been associated with measurement of the amount of fishing in terms of catch, and limited entry (licensing) in terms of some unit of fishing effort. These pairs have the greater immediate administrative convenience, but the opposite groupings—a quota measured, say, in number of voyages or licences to catch certain quantities of fish—are perfectly feasible, and may in the long run lead to rather fewer difficulties. A single effort quota does not in fact seem ever to be used, but the present Antarctic whaling régime is in effect through licences to catch fixed proportions of the permitted overall catch.

SINGLE QUOTA SYSTEMS

A single quota system appears to be simpler to operate than a licensing system, and has therefore usually been the first to be introduced when the amount of fishing in a multinational fishery has to be limited. Whatever the difficulties may be in such a fishery, for all the countries to agree that any increase in fishing beyond some specified limit should be prevented (which agreement is the essential preliminary to a single quota), it is far more difficult to reach agreement on what individual limitations should be accepted by each participating country, which is required before any system of licensing or limited entry is introduced. Assuming that the necessary calculations of the desired catch quota, taking into account year-class fluctuations, etc., or of the effort quotas, taking into account changes in efficiency, etc., have been done correctly, the desired fishing mortality will be exerted. So far as the purely biological objectives are concerned, the management should be successful. It is unlikely that the economic objectives will come so close to being fulfilled, and there is little chance in the long run that costs will be greatly reduced.

The reason is that, as has already been noted in connexion with management by closed seasons, any initial success in reducing costs will attract new entrants into the fishery, leading to the quota being reached earlier and earlier, a shorter open season, and increasingly inefficient operations for each vessel. This effect has been very clearly pointed out for the Pacific halibut fishery (Crutchfield and Zellner, 1963), but *Table* 6 shows the same thing happening in Antarctic whaling and in the Peruvian anchovy fishery. The same shortening of the open season has also occurred in the tuna fishery in the eastern tropical Pacific. In each case the controls set (by the International Pacific Halibut Commission, I.W.C., the Peruvian Government, or I.-A.T.T.C.) had no effect on the size or capacity of the fleets, which continued to increase after regulations were introduced. The amount of fishing was restricted (though not strictly enough in the case of whales), leading to an ever-decreasing open season. In the Antarctic the problem was solved by moving to an allocation system, though formally outside I.W.C. For the halibut a modification of the pattern of open seasons, and different regulations for different areas, had led to a rather longer effective open season, though this is still short compared with the normal season in the absence of regulation. A variety of measures are being implemented or considered by the Peruvian Government to reduce the excess capacity of the fleet, and to spread fishing more evenly through the year. So far the tuna regulations are in their early stages, and no way has been found to prevent the shortening season. Also in this case the economic pressures to do so are less, since the U.S.A. tuna seiners have alternative employment in the closed season for yellowfin, either fishing for skipjack in roughly the same area or moving to the Atlantic for yellowfin (and also skipjack). Their overhead costs can therefore be spread over these alternative fisheries, and a year's depreciation, maintenance, etc., does not have to be charged against three months' Pacific yellowfin fishing —though in fact the recent advances in purse-seining techniques for tuna have made this type of fishing so efficient that the vessels could still operate at a very good profit when fishing for a very few months in a year. This is why tuna boats were being built in such numbers in 1969–71, even when it was clear that as far as the yellowfin in the Eastern Pacific was concerned, more than enough boats were already taking part.

Table 6.—LENGTH OF OPEN SEASON (DAYS) IN SOME REGULATED FISHERIES IN WHICH THERE HAS BEEN NO CONTROL OF FLEET CAPACITY

| PACIFIC HALIBUT* | | ANTARCTIC WHALING | | PERUVIAN ANCHOVY‡ | |
Area 2	Area 3				
Year	Days	Days	Season	Days	Year	Days
1933	206	268	1945/46	121	1963	299
1934	172	241	1946/47	121	1963	269
1935	159	270	1947/48	115	1964	197
1936	148	233	1948/49	102	1965	165
1937	135	218	1949/50	84	1966	190
1938	120	212	1950/51	78	1967	170
1939	120	211	1951/52	64	1968	167
1940	104	179	1952/53	74	1969	162
1941	91	167	1953/54	76	1970	180
1942	75	163	1954/55	72	1971	89
1943	66	146	1955/56	58		
1944	51	194	1956/57	69		
1945	46	147	1957/58	69		
1946	42	111	1958/59	69		
1947	39	109	1959/60	102†		
1948	32	72	1960/61	101		
1949	34	73				
1950	32	66				

* *From* Crutchfield, 1962.

† Arrangements for division of the quota introduced in the 1959/60 Antarctic season.

‡ Number of days on which full fishing allowed. Limited amounts of fishing allowed for certain section of the fishery on other days.

In addition to the increasing costs of exerting the desired fishing mortality in the shortened season likely to arise with a single unallocated quota, the value of the catch may be reduced. In the Pacific halibut fishery the entire year's catch is landed in a few weeks. This means that virtually all of it has to be frozen and stored, adding to the costs of the necessary shore facilities as well as reducing the value of the catch—certainly at first-hand sale. The value to the consumer is also reduced slightly, since frozen halibut some months old is worth less than fresh halibut. The reduction in this case is likely to be small since the halibut market has traditionally been one for frozen fish, but the loss in value might be considerable in a product less suitable for long-term preservation.

If strict economic considerations are not important in choosing management objectives this shortening of the season may not be undesirable. The Pacific halibut fishery is conducted to a large extent by old vessels owned and crewed by even older fishermen. The present regulations discourage the entrance of new and efficient vessels—they specify that only longline gear may be used and it would be difficult to get a good return on new investment that can only be used for a short period. On the other hand a short fishing season is quite suitable for the part-time or semi-retired fishermen who make up an appreciable part of the U.S.A. fishery. For them, the regulations can not unreasonably be considered as a satisfying form of pension.

LIMITED ENTRY AND ALLOCATION

Providing a pension for fishermen and assuring the employment of the maximum number of fishermen are not among the most common objectives of management. For any other objective which normally requires reducing the real costs of harvesting, control limited to a single overall quota is unsatisfactory. It is particularly unsatisfactory in an international fishery where each country will have its own particular objective. With a single quota every country would have to adopt the same procedure of fishing as hard as possible with the maximum fleet or have its share of the total catch steadily decreased. A single quota, taken during a limited and decreasing fraction of the year is also likely to be inequitable as between fleets of different types of ships. A country with a fleet of large long-range vessels would be able to concentrate a large part of its total capacity on the stock being managed during the open season, and then used the ships elsewhere with little loss to overall efficiency. Another country with small local-based ships may have no alternative employment for them during the closed season. This possible inequity did not occur either in Antarctic whaling or Pacific halibut fishing, where all the participating countries had similar vessels. It is, however, a real problem in the tuna fishery in the eastern Pacific, where the larger seiners can move to other areas. Special provisions have had to be made for the smaller vessels to continue catching a limited quantity of yellowfin tuna after the main open season ends.

The solution to these difficulties, as has been pointed out clearly by several groups, such as the working group set up by the International Commission for the North-west Atlantic Fisheries (I.C.N.A.F., 1968), is to allocate specific shares of the total quota to each country. Each can then organize its own affairs so as to best fulfil its particular objective within the limits of the total national quota: one may make no further provision, allowing free fishing until the quota is taken, while another may issue a limited number of licences.

Such allocation immediately raises the question of how the division is to be made. The simplest is an equal split between all concerned. Though this cannot be widely applied, the International Pacific Salmon Fisheries Commission, which manages the large runs of the salmon to the Fraser River (which enters the sea in British Columbia just north of the U.S.A. border), is committed to ensuring that equal quantities are caught by U.S.A. and Canadian fishermen. However, this is achieved by juggling with the times at which different areas are open to fishing rather than by allocation as such.

A formula for allocation, or rather principles for guidelines for allocating, has been derived by I.C.N.A.F., This divides the total available quota into three parts. The smallest part is set aside to cover catches by non-participating countries, which for one reason or another are not members of the Commission—the country is just starting fishing in the region, or there are political objections to membership (East Germany, for example, is not a member of I.C.N.A.F.). This fraction must be small, otherwise it is doubtful whether the Commission's actions would be effective—probably no more than 5 per cent. The largest share, perhaps as much as 75–80 per cent, would be allocated in proportion to the past catches over perhaps the past five or ten years. If a country took 10 per cent of the total catch in that period, then it would be allocated 10

Table 7.—Percentage Composition of Total Fish Catches (in 000 tons) in the North-west Atlantic. (Data from I.C.N.A.F. Statistical Bulletin.)

Year	1963	1964	1965	1966	1967	1968	1969	1970	1971
Canada (N)*	18·1	18·1	17·3	20·0	19·7	20·4	19·6	21·4	21·1
Canada (M)*	10·7	9·9	9·6	10·5	11·4	11·8	12·9	14·4	12·9
Denmark	4·5	4·3	3·8	3·9	3·7	2·5	2·1	2·0	2·2
France	4·4	5·4	4·4	4·8	4·7	4·5	3·1	2·2	1·7
Germany, Fed. Rep. of	7·2	5·0	5·7	5·6	6·5	7·2	6·8	6·3	4·2
Iceland	0·5	0·3	0·3	0·2	0·1	0·1	0·2	—	0·1
Norway	1·5	1·7	1·4	1·3	1·8	1·5	1·5	1·4	1·1
Poland	0·8	1·3	1·8	2·3	3·6	4·8	4·3	5·2	5·4
Portugal	8·3	7·1	6·2	6·3	7·1	5·6	4·9	5·0	4·7
Spain	8·1	7·8	7·3	7·6	8·6	8·7	8·0	8·5	8·2
U.K.	1·5	1·8	1·7	1·9	2·4	1·2	0·2	0·2	0·2
U.S.A.	16·7	13·1	10·9	10·3	9·1	7·9	7·1	8·3	7·0
U.S.S.R.	17·7	20·9	26·7	22·3	17·2	19·0	23·6	21·7	28·0
Others†	0·1	3·3	3·0	3·1	4·3	4·7	(5·0)‡	(3·1)‡	(3·1)‡
Total Catch	2783	2952	3199	3189	3352	3901	3700‡	3265‡	3220‡

Note: * Canada (N) denotes Newfoundland and Labrador and (M) Maritimes and Quebec.
† Includes Romania and Japan, who became members of I.C.N.A.F. in 1967 and 1971, and East Germany.
‡ Estimated.

per cent of 80 per cent on the basis of historic performance. Finally, a proportion, perhaps 20 per cent, would be allocated according to special needs or interests. Such special allocation might be made to the state or states off whose shores the fish occur, and also to countries that are developing their fisheries. In the North-west Atlantic Poland has been building up her fleet steadily in recent years, so that her average catches in the past would underestimate the proportion of the total catch Polish vessels would be likely to catch in the future (*see Table 7*).

It can of course be claimed that since the need for management has arisen because the amount of fishing has increased beyond the desirable level, those countries (e.g., Poland) which are immediately responsible for this increase should bear the brunt of any reduction. Shares should be based on past performance at times when the effort was not too high, rather than on present or hypothetical future shares when there is too much fishing. A proposal along these lines, to omit from calculation of past performance years where 'overfishing' was taking place, was in fact put before I.C.N.A.F. by the U.S.A. delegation at its 1971 session.

Countries which are developing their fisheries, which are often the poorer and less well-developed countries in general economic matters, may however well feel that the fish resources of the high seas should not be reserved for those that happen to exploit them first. Some of the developing countries of Africa and Asia would go further and suggest that since fishing gives them one of the best opportunities for building up their protein supplies, while the rich countries have plenty of alternatives, the poorer countries should be given priority. In practice, whatever the general guidelines, the actual division in a particular case will be a matter of hard bargaining, in which external conditions with at most minor direct concern with management (e.g., port facilities) will be taken into account. Such bargaining would have much in common with the international commodity discussions in which, to maintain a reasonable balance of supply and demand, the world production of sugar or coffee is limited, with quotas allocated to each producing country—with not surprisingly a number of special arrangements outside the general systems. While the discussions on national catch quotas will be long and difficult the experience of these commodity arrangements, and of the division of the Antarctic whale quota between such diverse countries as Norway, Japan, and U.S.S.R., show that it is possible to reach agreement.

NATIONAL LICENSING

Given a national share of an international fishery, or a defined level of fishing in a purely national fishery, there are a number of ways of achieving the objective. While the target will be defined as a given amount of fishing, measured either as so much catch or as nominal fishing effort, the ultimate objective—high catch at low cost—will be better achieved by aiming at a reduction of the fishing capacity. The capacity may be defined as the fishing mortality (or the catch or fishing effort) which can be caused by the fleet concerned during a year of fishing season, if it fished freely without restrictions imposed for reasons of conservation. It is a rather less precise term than 'mortality' or 'effort'. A long-range fleet can be easily diverted from one stock to another so that its capacity is not easily definable with reference to a single stock; for instance, the English distant water fleet has no unique capacity as far as, say, cod stocks at West Greenland are concerned—their catches from there may vary from nearly zero to up to a fifth of the total. It is meaningful, though, to consider the English distant water capacity for all the North Atlantic cod stocks, considered as a whole. Russians, however, have fewer prejudices against anything that is not cod—or perhaps better control over the consumer—and their long-range capacity is more or less world-wide.

Even for local fleets, restricted to a single stock, a given capacity—a given number of ships of a certain type—would exert a different mortality, in effect take a different catch, from year to year in accordance with changes in the distribution and migrations of the stocks, and changes in the overall abundance of the stock. The latter will obviously affect the catch, but is also likely to change the mortality—the more fish there are, the more time will be spent handling the fish, or steaming to and from the grounds, and less time will be spent actually fishing, or looking for fish. Control of capacity alone is therefore unlikely to ensure the correct mortality. However, if the capacity is brought into reasonable accord with the desired fishing mortality, i.e., the available capacity is such that the mortality will just be achieved during a season when conditions are unusually unfavourable—the fish dispersed or otherwise difficult to catch—then supplementary regulations, such as a short closed season, to keep the fishing mortality at the desired level, will have only a small impact and be easy to enforce.

Keeping the capacity at the desired level needs some type of licensing or limited entry system. Most countries require fishing vessels to be licensed. Normally the licence fee, if one exists, is purely nominal, covering only the administrative costs. Also licences are often granted to all those who apply for them, which may be more than the desirable number. The case of licensing as a management tool to keep the capacity at the optimum level is not common. The most important example is that of the Japanese high seas fisheries, in which the numbers of licences is adjusted to the potential of the resource. Where the resource is valuable and easily harvested, as in the high seas salmon fishery, the licences are very valuable, and there is considerable pressure to obtain a licence or in some way to get round the licensing system. The attempted entry by the Republic of Korea into the high seas salmon fishery was partially backed by Japanese firms unable to obtain a licence for themselves.

Another example of a licence scheme which was highly successful, at least in the past, was the South and South-west Africa shoal fish fishery (Gertenbach, 1962). Here the licences were used to control both the capacity, ashore and afloat, and the actual catch each year. Each factory was allowed to process a certain quantity of fish, which was adjusted from time to time in accordance with the knowledge of the stocks (and also with commercial and economic pressures), and to operate a certain number and size of vessels. This scheme has been in risk of being destroyed by its own success. The profits of those having licences were so high (of the order of 50 per cent of annual turnover in good seasons), that there was great pressure for new licences to be issued or to find a way around the licence system altogether. This was found by the operation of converted whale factory ships, which, supplied by fleets of small purse-seiners, processed the fish into fish meal while beyond territorial limits. It seems that the great increase in effort which occurred around 1970 due to the operations of these vessels and to additional licences for shore operations, have had a serious effect on the stocks but this does not invalidate the success of the licensing scheme while it was properly enforced.

A slightly different situation is arising in British Columbia where a licensing system is being introduced to rationalize the numerous, but generally inefficient, salmon fishery—the inefficiency being in a large part due to the complex management measures applied to control the large over-capacity. Numerically a large part of the fleet was vessels which fished only intermittently for salmon, and accordingly two types of licences were issued—

B for these part-time fishermen considered as vessels landing less than $1250 worth of salmon in the base years (1967 or 1968), and A licences for the others. Class B licences are issued only for the life of the vessel, which could not be replaced. Class A licences can be sold, and the vessel be replaced by another—which is the only way a new vessel can enter the fleet.

An important feature of the British Columbia scheme is that the licence fee for Class A boats is not nominal; in 1971, the third year of the scheme, it was $200–$400, with the likelihood that it would be increased as reduced fleet capacity leads to better profits for those remaining in the fishery. The present intention is that licence fees will be used to finance a 'buy-back' scheme under which A licences can be surrendered to the Government. Through this buy-back scheme, and the natural attrition of the Class B licences, it is expected that the fleet will be reduced to somewhat more manageable numbers. Some quite appreciable reduction has already been achieved, but since the vessels leaving have been those that caught very few salmon the effective reduction in fleet capacity is so far still small. Ultimately the capacity should be reduced to something more commensurate with the magnitude of the resource, so that the harvesting can be done in the most efficient manner for the benefit, in proportions apparently yet to be decided, of the fishermen, the consumer, and the Government.

The British Columbia case represents a step towards the ultimate economic method of licence allocation, which is simply by recourse to market factors. The cost of licences is increased until the number of applications for licences ceases to exceed the number that is to be issued. At that point the difficult political decision on who is to have licences, and who not, is eliminated. If licences are issued in the same units as those in which the target figure (quota) of fishing mortality is measured, e.g. licences to land some fixed quantity of fish, no additional regulation is needed. It may be more convenient to issue a licence to operate a given ship, the licence fee perhaps being calculated on the basis of so much per gross ton. Then, using the licences to keep the fleet capacity within appropriate limits, additional regulations would probably be needed each year as a fine control to keep the mortality at the right level, e.g. by stopping the fishing when the seasonal catch quota has been achieved. If the capacity has been properly controlled this closure will not occur until near the end of the normal season, and little inefficiency will result.

REFERENCES

BEVERTON, R. J. H., and HOLT, S. J. (1957), 'On the dynamics of exploited fish populations', *Fish. Invest. Lond.*, ser. 2, **19**, 533.

BEVERTON, R. J. H., and HODDER, V. M. (1962), 'Report of the working group of scientists on fishery assessment in relation to regulation problems', *Ann. Proc. int. Commn. N.W. Atlant. Fish.*, **11**, suppl.

BOEREMA, L. K., SAETERSDAL, G., and VALDIVIA, J. E. (1965), 'Report on the effects of fishing on the Peruvian stock of anchoveta', *F.A.O. Fish. Tech. Pap.*, 55.

BOWEN, B. K. (1963), 'Preliminary report on the effectiveness of escape gaps', *W. Austral. Fish. Dept. Rept.* 2, 1–19.

BOWEN, B. K. (1971), 'Management of western rock lobster (*Panulirus longipes cygnus* George)', *Proc. Indo-Pacific Fish. Counc.* 14th Session, sect. 2, 139–153.

CRUTCHFIELD, J. A. (1962), 'Regulation of the Pacific coast halibut fishery', *F.A.O. Fish. Rep.*, **5**, 353–92.

CRUTCHFIELD, J. A., and ZELLNER, A. (1963), 'Economic aspects of the Pacific halibut fishery', *Fish. indust. Res.*, **1**, No. 1.

CRUTCHFIELD, J. A., and PONTECORVO, G. (1969), *The Pacific Salmon Fisheries. A Study of Irrational Conservation.* Baltimore: Johns Hopkins Press.

GERTENBACH, L. P. D. (1962), 'Regulation of the South African west coast shoal fisheries', *F.A.O. Fish. Rep.*, **5**, 427–60.

GRAHAM, H. W. (1954), 'Conserving New England haddock', *Trans. 19th N. Am. Wildlife Conf.*, 397–402.

GULLAND, J. A. (1956), 'On the fishing effort in English demersal fisheries', *Fish. Invest., Lond.*, ser. 2, **20**(5).

GULLAND, J. A. (1961), 'The estimation of the effect on catches of changes in gear selectivity', *J. Cons. int. Explor. Mer*, **26**(2), 204–14.

GULLAND, J. A. (1964), 'Variations in selection factors and mesh differentials', *J. Cons. int. Explor. Mer*, **29**(1), 61–64.

GULLAND, J. A. (1968), 'Recent changes in the North Sea plaice fishery', *J. Cons. int. Explor. Mer*, **31**(3), 305–22.

HIGH, W. L., ELLIS, I. E., and LUSZ, L. D. (1969), 'A progress report on the development of a shrimp trawl to separate shrimp from fish and bottom dwelling animals', *Comm. Fish Rev.*, March, 20–33.

ROBSON, D. S. (1966), 'Estimation of the relative fishing power of individual ships', *Res. Bull. int. Comm. N.W. Atlant. Fish.*, **3**, 5–14.

SHINDO, S. (1971), 'On the fisheries management in the East China Sea and Yellow Sea', *Proc. Indo-Pacific Fish. Counc.*, 14th Session, sect. 2, 92–104.

TÅNING, A. V. (ed.) (1948), 'Northwestern area Committee: report of the sub-committee on Faxa Bay', *Rapp. Proc. Verb. Cons. int. Explor. Mer*, **120**, 129.

Chapter

7

THE MECHANICS OF
INTERNATIONAL FISHERY MANAGEMENT

WHATEVER the desired objectives of management, and whatever
the measures chosen to achieve the objectives, some machinery is
needed to bring these measures into effect. In a purely national
fishery this machinery can be part of the normal administration
and no special arrangements are necessary. In the multi-national
fisheries, which include most of the major fisheries in the world,
some new formal arrangements are usually needed. During the
last few years, with the growth of world fisheries, and especially
the growth of long-range fisheries involving several countries
exploiting the same stock, there has been a steady growth in the
various international bodies with various responsibilities in the
field of fishery management.

These responsibilities are varied, and the subjects covered
include biological studies, to determine what is happening to the
stocks, and what the effects on the fish stocks and subsequent catches would be of possible measures; economic and
social studies to determine the best practical choice between
different possible measures; formal negotiations to reach agreement on the measures which should be taken, and arrangements
for mutual inspection, or some other method of assurance
that the measures are in fact being carried out by all
concerned.

These different responsibilities require a variety of different
types of arrangement, and of participation by the countries
concerned. The final and vital steps of actually putting management measures into effect, together with the necessary enforcement
and inspection procedures, will require full participation by virtually all countries. Any management scheme must imply some
degree of restriction on the fishermen, and if only fishermen from

some countries are affected, they will suffer for the benefit of the others, and the whole management scheme will be short-lived, if indeed it ever came into effect.

On the other hand the scientific assessment of the state of the stocks requires assembly of the necessary data and its study by the most competent scientists available. It is not essential that representatives from all countries take part in the evaluation—and indeed it is highly desirable that the scientists should not, during the scientific discussions, consider themselves as national representatives—though it is necessary that all countries should be willing to accept the results of the scientists' deliberations as providing the agreed basis of action. Sometimes it is suggested that the scientific advice on management should be provided by a completely independent scientific body, not likely to be prejudiced by particular national viewpoints. This would certainly be a fine procedure if the independent scientists had sufficient data and ability in all cases to assess the stock with perfect precision, and to determine the unique best procedure for management. In practice the data is rarely as complete or as up-to-date as would be needed, and important scientific questions—such as the relation between the size of the adult stock and subsequent recruitment—remain for most stocks unresolved. The scientific advice about any particular stock is therefore likely to be hedged about with a collection of possible alternatives and qualifications. It is then desirable that the process of deciding on the measures taken should be closely integrated with that of producing the scientific assessments. Nevertheless it is convenient to discuss the two stages separately.

PROVISION OF SCIENTIFIC ADVICE

Arrangements for international study of the fish stocks are not only logically the first step to be discussed, but are also historically the first for which permanent formal arrangements were set up. The International Council for the Exploration of the Sea, whose headquarters are in Copenhagen, was set up in 1902 (a further Convention, giving I.C.E.S. a more formal constitution was signed in 1964), and since then has been responsible for co-ordinating and stimulating marine research in the North-east Atlantic (strictly, under the 1964 convention, the Atlantic Ocean and adjacent seas, though on the one hand its attention has been concentrated on the North Sea and nearby waters, and on the other the authority of I.C.E.S. has given it an influence on marine research in all parts of the world).

I.C.E.S. is the perfect example of how scientists would like to arrange their work. In its golden age, up to the second world war, it was essentially a club to which belonged all members of the small group of scientists engaged in the study of the open seas (among which fishery biologists were a large part). A very considerable proportion of these could come together each autumn at the annual meeting of I.C.E.S. to discuss the results of the past summer's work at sea and to make plans for the next year. As the numbers of marine scientists around the North Sea have increased from a few dozen to some hundreds, the meetings have become more formal and the opportunities of the younger scientist to attend regularly are now small. The club atmosphere remains, and is a great advantage when working on the difficult scientific problems arising in relation to many fish stocks.

The importance of I.C.E.S. is more than just the provision of a friendly atmosphere. It has also been a leader in the two major steps in providing scientific advice—first, the compilation and publication of detailed statistics; and, secondly, bringing together the small group of those with direct expert knowledge of the assessment of the stock of fish being considered in order to prepare a report on the state of that stock. The statistics date back to the foundation of I.C.E.S., and (with some discontinuity during each war) the annual *Bulletin Statistique* of I.C.E.S. has given, for each year since 1906, the total catch of each species, by each country in each of the statistical areas of I.C.E.S. In addition, in the last couple of decades I.C.E.S. has produced, in its *Statistical Newsletter*, both more detailed data of catches and corresponding fishing effort by small areas (most often by approximately thirty-mile squares, of $1°$ latitude by $\frac{1}{2}°$ longitude), and data on the length or size composition of samples of catches.

These are the basic raw materials of any assessment. Whatever the precise regional arrangements for scientific study, one of the first steps must be to ensure the collection and tabulation of such data. An important aspect is that they must be comprehensive. Catch statistics are at best of little value, and can easily be badly misleading, unless all the catches from the stock are included, by whatever country they are taken. Data on fishing effort, and also on the size composition of the fish caught need not be so comprehensive, since extrapolation from one country to another is not so difficult. If German trawlers catch twice as much cod off western Greenland as English trawlers their fishing effort must be twice as great—though their number of hours fishing may be more or less than precisely twice the number of hours fishing by English trawlers, depending on the relative fishing power of the typical vessel in the two national fleets.

The size composition of the catches of fish by one country cannot be so unequivocally determined from catches of another country since differences in the type of gear used, and in the main times and places of fishing, and, indirectly, in the market preferences, will result in often quite marked differences in the sizes of fish taken by different countries from the same stock. However, reasonable estimates can often be made. Thus the I.C.N.A.F. assessment group (Beverton and Hodder, 1962) could identify, for the several countries fishing at West Greenland which did not sample their catches to estimate the sizes of fish caught, a fishery of another country for which samples were available, and whose catches by reason of the similarity in gear used, market demand, etc., could be reasonably supposed to have a similar size composition.

In some other regions of the world arrangements roughly similar to those made by I.C.E.S. in the North-east Atlantic are in existence for the provision of comprehensive catch statistics, that is, there exists some central agency which compiles and publishes a bulletin from the statistics provided by the various countries. The arrangements in the North-west Atlantic where the I.C.N.A.F. has published its detailed *Statistical Bulletin* for each year since 1950 are almost exactly the same. In several other areas, e.g., in the Eastern Central Atlantic, F.A.O. on behalf of its various regional bodies (e.g., the Fishery Committee for the Eastern Central Atlantic, C.E.C.A.F.), is beginning to compile similar bulletins. So far as the Atlantic statistics are concerned the work by the national statistical offices is lightened as far as possible by the three organizations—F.A.O., I.C.E.S., and I.C.N.A.F.—using a common system and standard forms for reporting statistics.

In principle the formal arrangements for this work are minimal —a reasonably efficient postal system, and a few clerks with adding machines (or in the modern age fewer clerks, but an access to computers) in the central office. Reporting must be complete, or virtually complete, but there is no need for all countries to be formally members of the central organization. The U.S.S.R., for example, is not a member of F.A.O., but by reason of her widespread fishing activities gives a more voluminous statistical report to F.A.O. than any member country. The biggest procedural difficulty has arisen when political relations are so strained that the assistance of one country cannot easily be acknowledged by another. I.C.N.A.F. has long included the catches by the German Democratic Republic under 'Non-member Countries', to avoid insulting one or other Germany (the Federal Republic of Germany is a member of I.C.N.A.F.), by using an inappropriate title. This problem is small, and the harder problem awaits the compiler of the first regional statistics for the Yellow Sea, and the East China Sea, where the major fishery nations are Japan, Taiwan, Republic of China, North Korea, and the Republic of Korea.

A problem of a practical, rather than a political nature, is that this system assumes good national statistics, which can be a rash assumption. The solution then is for the central agency to take on the job of collecting (rather than merely compiling) the statistics. This is done by the Inter-American Tropical Tuna Commission, which has its headquarters in southern California, the home of the U.S. purse-seine fleet which is much the largest fleet operating in the Commission's area (the eastern tropical Pacific). The skippers of the large purse-seiners complete a detailed log-book during each trip, which is handed to an agent of the Commission on return to port. Other agents are based in ports in Latin American countries where significant quantities of tuna are landed and they collect data from the vessels as they land. This system is expensive, though undoubtedly highly effective in getting the information required, and getting it with the precision and detail required. Collecting statistics in this way is also likely to be particularly desirable (if still too costly in many cases) when management measures, especially those involving limitations of the catch, are in operation. In practice nearly all central agencies have to rely on national systems for collecting the basic statistical material. The agencies (including various Commissions charged with direct responsibility for management) have to limit themselves with urging the countries to provide the necessary data and expediting this by specifying precisely what data is required. While most international conventions concerned with fishery management require countries to carry out management measures and most call upon either the countries, or some international commission, to carry out research, including the compilation of statistics, few explicitly call upon countries to provide the necessary statistics. Significantly an exception is the latest Convention, that for the conservation of Antarctic seals, signed in London in February, 1972, which spells out in some detail the statistical and routine biological data to be supplied by an contracting party which engages in commercial sealing in the Antarctic. It is to be hoped that this will become a generally accepted principle—that any country exploiting a high-seas fishery resource must supply to the appropriate authority specified statistical data, e.g., total catch, by species, area, and period, with the corresponding data on the fishing effort, and also information on the size composition of the fish caught.

The Preparation of Scientific Reports to Managers

Given good basic information, the next step is to analyse it to determine the state of the stock—essentially the shape of the yield curves (or yield as a function of the amount of fishing, and, if relevant, of yield as a function of size at first capture) and the present position of the fishery on them. The need is for a single, compact report that gives the agreed views of all the scientists concerned, and which can be used as the basis of the subsequent discussions on the measures to be introduced. Without such an agreed statement it is inevitable that in any situation with any significant divergence of interests (or even of apparent interests), arguments on scientific matters will be raised in the political discussions. Since agreement among the industries and administrators is often difficult enough when restricted to non-scientific matters, the addition of an extra field of possible argument makes the likelihood of early agreement (and often effective and painless action) that much smaller.

That is not to say that it is necessary for the scientists to be in complete agreement. Indeed if there are more than one or two scientists actively engaged in a problem it is highly unlikely that such agreement will exist on all points. What is possible is to agree on a report to the management authority which sets out the aspects on which there is agreement, and the various divergences. This report should follow through the consequences of the different interpretation of the data, when they exist, to point out the consequences in terms of the results of management action. Often there can be quite sharp differences on scientific points without affecting the conclusions as to the action to be taken. Thus when the Committee of Three were preparing their report on

Antarctic Whaling (Chapman, 1964) there was uncertainty on the growth-rate of whales—layers could be counted on the wax plugs in the ears, but it was not known whether one layer or two were laid down each year. This made some difference to the estimate of the time that would be taken for the stocks to rebuild after appropriate measures were taken to restrict catches, but the conclusions about the desirable immediate action would be unaltered—catches had to be quickly and drastically reduced.

Even when there is some difference in the best action that should be taken, according to which scientific analysis is correct, there may be a lack of symmetry in the situation which may leave little doubt as to the action that should be taken by any prudent man. Again, the Antarctic whales provide a good example. Even as late as 1962 one or two scientists were claiming that the fin whale stock had not been reduced, or at least was not conclusively proved to have been reduced. If this belief were accepted, there would still have been little if any loss in reducing catches for a few years while better assessments were forthcoming—catches could have been correspondingly increased for a few years thereafter. However, if the alternative, more pessimistic, and as it has turned out more correct, hypothesis of a serious decline in the fin whale stock was right, only a substantial reduction in catch would avert the near commercial extinction of the stock. Faced with these alternatives, there would seem to be only one rational course of action. Unfortunately the Whaling Commission was not given advice in this detail, and the wrong action was pursued for too long.

Since the scientific advice to the management body (International Commission or other organization) has to be carefully formulated with the needs of the Commission in mind, the most direct method is for it to be provided by the staff of the Commission itself. This is done by several Commissions in western North America (e.g., the Inter-American Tropical Tuna Commission, and the International Pacific Halibut Commission), and certainly has resulted in these bodies being provided with scientific advice that is well suited to their needs. Also, perhaps most notably in the case of the Tuna Commission, it has resulted in scientific studies of considerable significance in their own right.

These arrangements, however, suffer from a number of disadvantages. Possibly the most obvious is concerning finance. Research is seldom cheap, and the annual budget of Commissions with their own research staff is an order of magnitude greater, on the average, than those of bodies relying on national research. While it is by no means certain that this would not be the cheapest and most effective way of having the necessary research carried out, most governments or politicians have a not un-natural prejudice against giving money to some international organization over which they have little direct control, and are much happier giving the same, or even rather more, money to their own national research institutes. International bodies therefore find it difficult to obtain the funds to carry out research in the breadth and detail that is desirable as the foundation of management decisions.

The opposite arrangement is epitomized by I.C.E.S. and its arrangements with the North-east Atlantic Fisheries Commission. Here the research is entirely carried out by scientists in various national institutions. As scientific problems arise in N.E.A.F.C., the management body, these are referred to I.C.E.S., and in the first instance dealt with by its Liaison Committee. If the problems are of any substance they are normally dealt with by setting up a working group of scientists from the various national laboratories with any knowledge of information about the question, to put all this information together.

This system has worked very well. Not only does it normally result in a single agreed piece of scientific advice, on which the Commission can act, but this advice is usually better than could be provided by any one scientist or laboratory working alone. One reason is that as far as possible all the basic data is brought together—though when such working groups were a less familiar part of the fishery scientist's world there was some difficulty to persuade a few scientists to disinter material on, for example, detailed catch statistics over the past twenty years which had been awaiting use in preparing an extensive monograph on the species concerned. This is an off-shoot of the scientific form of the modern rat-race in which volume of publication over one's name is an accepted measure of scientific worth. People have now learned that the general advantage of putting all the basic information on the table outweighs any loss in personal publication—and in fact the wider availability of data improves these publications. Another advantage is that the working groups can include a variety of detailed expertise. Thus in a group studying the Arctic cod, the Norwegian scientists brought extensive knowledge of the biology of the adult fish, especially in relation to the spawning in the Lofoten Islands; the Russians, knowledge of the younger fish, especially on the year-to-year changes in the abundance and distribution of the one- to four-year-old fish, before they enter the fishery; while the English contributed their expertise on the mathematical aspects of population dynamics.

However, in its present form, with any international body performing no more than the simplest secretarial role, this system too has its weaknesses. These are mostly concerned with the shortage of the ideal expert for this work, who can understand all the complexities of the scientific studies, pick out the essential points which are directly relevant to management problems, and set these out clearly so that the administrators can make their decisions. In the absence of the perfect team, or even of acceptable substitutes, the report of a working group deals too much with irrelevant, though interesting, scientific details, and no clear message gets through. Since the techniques and problems are common to many situations much is gained by someone attending all working groups, and carrying out, before the actual meeting, some of the routine analyses, as well as guiding the discussions, and ultimately the report, along lines likely to be helpful to the users. Thus I.C.E.S. have appointed a staff member to act as secretary to the Liaison Committee, and to its associated working groups.

If the need for central guidance and assistance is necessary in I.C.E.S., and also I.C.N.A.F., when the member countries are all rich developed countries of Europe and North America (recently also Japan has joined I.C.N.A.F.) which might be presumed each to have its own competent research organizations, it is obviously still more necessary in other regions where many of the countries actually or potentially participating in the fisheries are small and poor. The need is twofold—brought about partly by an overall shortage of experise and partly by an imbalance of the supply of what expertise there is. It may be, in considering, for example, the state of the tuna stocks in the Indian Ocean, that the only scientists active in studying those resources are scientists in Japan and Korea, whose fishermen have dominated the fishery for a decade. Further, these scientists may produce a report that is in no way biased by the interests of Japanese or Korean fishermen. It is still very difficult to persuade, say, Indian fishermen of this lack of bias if the scientific report implies the need to discourage further new fishing for tuna in the Indian Ocean, and this suspicion can add significantly to the problems of acting on the scientific results. These doubts can be largely resolved if in addition to the national participants in any working group, there are also one or two independent experts, who can, as well as contributing their personal expertise, ensure that the interests of the smaller or poorer countries are not overlooked. A compromise pattern with contributions from national and independent scientists is becoming a common pattern, and may well turn out to be the best solution.

ECONOMIC ANALYSIS

The arrangements discussed in the previous section cover mainly advice on the scientific situation, or often more strictly, the biological analysis. Although it is frequently implied that management decisions should be made purely on objective, scientific grounds, only exceptionally will the biological evidence point uniquely to a particular action. Thus in 1963 there was no doubt that an immediate and drastic reduction in Antarctic whale catches was essential. Now the best action in Antarctic whaling is less clear, particularly as regards fin whales. Future catches could undoubtedly be increased if the fin whale stocks were allowed to re-build, and the rate of this recovery, and the total long-term catches, would be maximized if present catches were cut to zero. However, the rate of recovery is slow, and it would not require an outrageously high discount rate to make the long-term gain barely equal to the immediate sacrifices. Certainly the choice of any intermediate position, involving a moderate decrease in catches and a less than maximal recovery rate, involves economic rather than biological considerations. Probably the most rational programme on economic and practical grounds would be to allow the present whaling equipment (which is not well suited for any other purpose) to continue operations during the rest of its technically effective life, but to allow the stocks to be rebuilt before investing in new equipment.

A major reason for the neglect, in the international scheme, of economic factors, and for the common omission of any formal arrangements for getting economic advice, has been the presumed differences between countries. Thus the biological situation of, say, the cod off West Greenland is the same whether it is considered from a German, a Danish (Greenlandic), or Portuguese viewpoint, but the economic assessment would depend on one's point of view. It is therefore possible to prepare a single international report dealing with the biological assessments, but economic analyses would need to be prepared on a country-by-country basis. Although strictly this is true, the economic differences between countries can be exaggerated. All countries would be pleased to catch the same amount of fish with less fishing. One exception to this only emphasizes the generality of the rule—in Greenland there is very little, if any, alternative occupation. If the fishermen are not fishing they are likely to be drinking, and even taking into account the running costs of the boats it may in the short run be cheaper to have the men at sea than idle ashore.

In general, though, the broad economic aspects of regulation and the potential benefits from sensible management actions are similar for all countries. It is therefore both possible and useful for a single review of the economic aspects to be prepared, either by national experts, or by some independent body, in the same way as the biological review. In fact it is often convenient for their economic review to be combined with the biological study, since on the one hand the biggest unresolved questions in the economic study are likely to arise from uncertainties in the biological analyses (e.g., what is the relation between stock and recruitment, and therefore what are the chances of there being a drastic fall in catch from too heavy fishing), and on the other hand the economic discussion should help draw out more clearly to the non-scientific audience the significant points in the biological study. Thus I.C.N.A.F. (1968) set up a joint group of biologists and economists to study the fisheries in the North-west Atlantic.

The extent of economic studies needed at the international level is, however, likely to be significantly less than for biological studies. The latter can be carried to great detail, but the detailed economic studies are more matters of national interest. While the broad studies will show a general economic benefit to all countries from reducing the amount of fishing, the detailed conclusions as to the best pattern of reduction will vary from one country to another. A country with a fleet of old, fully depreciated vessels and plenty of alternative employment for the fishermen, will be much more willing to consider an immediate cut in the amount of fishing on some given stock than another country which has just completed a new fleet of vessels specially designed for harvesting that stock, and with little alternative employment. There is therefore no great need for any large permanent structure to arrange for economic studies and for the provision of some review of the economic implications of possible management actions. In practice they can usually be handled by the same machinery as used for biological studies.

The Choice of Action

The step requiring the most formal international machinery is that of choosing the action to be taken. In a purely national fishery this can be a simple executive decision of the senior government officials concerned with fisheries. When more than one country is concerned, it is essential that any proposed action is followed by all, or virtually all, the participants in the fishery. Otherwise most if not all the benefits will go to those who do not abide by the proposed management action. There must therefore be arrangements, first for discussions by all parties to agree on the measures to be taken, and then for these measures to become, to some degree or other, a binding commitment for each country.

In principle these could be achieved by *ad hoc* conferences called to discuss some specific course of action. Indeed this is what happened during the pre-war period in relation to whales, where measures, e.g., on size limits and protection of whales with calves, were agreed. However, management should be a continuously evolving process, with changes in the pattern of fishing or in the scientific understanding of the stocks eliciting appropriate modifications in the management measures applied. This requires some permanent machinery. The result is the international fishery commissions of one type or another, whose numbers are steadily increasing as the need for management becomes better understood, and stocks of fish of more kinds and in more areas become heavily exploited and in need of management (*see Tables* 8a, 8b).

These Commissions differ in the power and authority for taking decisions that each body, and its staff, possess. Naturally the greatest power has been given to those bodies to which only a few countries of similar interests belong, and which have a strong permanent staff. This means in practice the species-based commissions of western North America. A good example of a body with strong authority is the International Pacific Salmon Fisheries Commission, dealing with the salmon which spawn in the Fraser River, which enters the Pacific near Vancouver.

The very great year-to-year variations in the number of salmon in the run, and in the precise migration patterns and timing of the runs make year-to-year adjustments in the management policies

Table 8a.—INTERNATIONAL BODIES CONCERNED WITH FISHERY MANAGEMENT, WITH ACRONYMS AND 1972 MEMBERSHIP.

B.S.S.S.C. (Baltic Sea Salmon Standing Committee)
Members: Denmark, Fed. Rep. Germany, Poland, Sweden.
C.A.R.P.A.S. (Regional Fisheries Advisory Commission for the South-West Atlantic)
Members: Argentina, Brazil, Uruguay.
C.E.C.A.F. (F.A.O. Fishery Committee for the Eastern Central Atlantic)
Members: Cameroon, Congo, Cuba, Dahomey, France, Gabon, Gambia, Ghana, Greece, Guinea, Italy, Ivory Coast, Japan, Korea, Liberia, Mauritania, Morocco, Nigeria, Poland, Romania, Senegal, Sierra Leone, Spain, Togo, U.K., U.S.A., Zaïre.
G.F.C.M. (General Fisheries Council for the Mediterranean)
Members: Algeria, Bulgaria, Cyprus, Egypt, France, Greece, Israel, Italy, Lebanon, Libya, Malta, Monaco, Morocco, Romania, Spain, Tunisia, Turkey, Yugoslavia.
I.A.T.T.C. (Inter-American Tropical Tuna Commission)
Members: Canada, Costa Rica, Japan, Mexico, Panama, U.S.A.
I.C.C.A.T. (International Commission for the Conservation of Atlantic Tunas)
Members: Brazil, Canada, France, Ghana, Japan, Korea, Morocco, Portugal, Senegal, South Africa, Spain, U.S.A.
I.C.N.A.F. (International Commission for the North-west Atlantic Fisheries)
Members: Canada, Denmark, France, Fed. Rep. Germany, Iceland, Italy, Japan, Norway, Poland, Portugal, Romania, Spain, U.K., U.S.A., U.S.S.R.
I.C.S.E.A.F. (International Commission for the South-East Atlantic Fisheries)
Members: Japan, Poland, Portugal, South Africa, Spain, U.S.S.R.
I.N.P.F.C. (International North Pacific Fisheries Commission)
Members: Canada, Japan, U.S.A.
I.O.F.C. (Indian Ocean Fisheries Commission)
Members: Australia, Bahrain, Ceylon, Cuba, Ethiopia, France, Greece, India, Indonesia, Iraq, Israel, Japan, Jordan, Kenya, Korea, Kuwait, Madagascar, Malaysia, Mauritius, Netherlands, Oman, Pakistan, Portugal, Qatar, Tanzania, Thailand, U.K., U.S.A., Vietnam.
I.P.F.C. (Indo-Pacific Fisheries Council)
Members: Australia, Burma, Ceylon, France, India, Indonesia, Japan, Khmer, Korea, Malaysia, Netherlands, New Zealand, Pakistan, Philippines, Thailand, U.K., U.S.A., Vietnam.
I.P.H.C. (International Pacific Halibut Commission)
Members: Canada, U.S.A.
I.P.S.F.C. (International Pacific Salmon Fisheries Commission)
Members: Canada, U.S.A.
I.W.C. (International Whaling Commission)
Members: Argentina, Australia, Canada, Denmark, France, Iceland, Japan, Mexico, Norway, Panama, South Africa, U.K., U.S.A., U.S.S.R.
J.K.F.C. (Japan–Republic of Korea Joint Fisheries Commission)
Members: Japan, Korea.
J.S.F.C. (Japanese–Soviet Fisheries Commission for the North-west Pacific)
Members: Japan, U.S.S.R.

M.C.B.S.F.   (Mixed Commission for Black Sea Fisheries)
  Members: Bulgaria, Romania, U.S.S.R.
N.E.A.F.C.   (North-East Atlantic Fisheries Commission)
  Members: Belgium, Denmark, France, Fed. Rep. Germany, Iceland,
              Ireland, Netherlands, Norway, Poland, Portugal, Spain, Sweden,
              U.K., U.S.S.R.
N.P.F.S.C.   (North Pacific Fur Seal Commission)
  Members: Canada, Japan, U.S.A., U.S.S.R.
P.C.S.P.   (Permanent Commission of the Conference on the Use and
              Conservation of the Marine Resources of the South Pacific)
  Members: Chile, Ecuador, Peru.
S.C.N.E.A.   (Sealing Commission for the North-East Atlantic)
  Members: Norway, U.S.S.R.
S.C.S.K.   (Shellfish Commission for the Skagerak-Kattegat)
  Members: Denmark, Norway, Sweden.

(Data on *Tables* 8*a* and 8*b* from F.A.O., 1972, Report on Regulatory Fishery
Bodies, F.A.O. Fisheries Circular 138.)

---

necessary. At the same time the very short season as the salmon
pass through the coastal fishing area on their way upstream from
their open-ocean feeding grounds make it necessary to implement
these adjustments very quickly, with a gap of at most a very few
days between the evidence on the condition of the run becoming
apparent in the magnitude and distribution of the catches, and
the resultant modification to the regulations being brought into
force. This speed of action cannot be achieved through detailed
international discussions. Decisions of this type have to be taken
by one man, willing to be proved wrong on occasion, provided that
over the years he has been right often enough.

The responsibility of the two countries concerned (U.S.A. and
Canada) is, on the basis of appropriate discussion, to give the one
man the necessary authority, and sufficient general instructions at
the beginning of each season on the policy he should follow.

Formally this is done at a meeting of the Commission attended
by three Commissioners from each country, usually representing
federal, state or provincial, and industrial interests, though the
discussion and formal voting at such meetings are normally pre-
ceded by other hearings with the general fisheries public at which
the policy of the Commission's staff is explained.

The opposite approach is one in which the rules and regulations
are carefully set out in detail at the formal meeting of the Commission, and only a minimum of flexibility is left to the Commission's staff. A clear example is the International Whaling
Commission, in which attached to the formal Convention setting

Table 8b.—Summary of Information on Regulatory Fishery Bodies.

Body	Date Established and Auspices	Headquarters	Eligibility for Membership	Area of Competence	Resources Covered	Functions
B.S.S.S.C.	1962 International Convention	Meets in member countries in rotation	Signatory States and others by unanimous agreement of Contracting Parties	Baltic Sea, including Gulf of Bothnia and Gulf of Finland	Salmon (*Salmo salar*)	To foster the development of salmon stocks, fish-breeding methods, and the rational exploitation of the salmon population
C.A.R.P.A.S.	1961 Resolution of F.A.O. Conference under Article VI-1 of F.A.O. Constitution	Rio de Janeiro, Brazil	F.A.O. Member Nations whose territory borders on Western Atlantic south of Equator	South-west Atlantic	All	To develop organized approach in respect of rational exploitation of resources; to encourage cooperative investigations
C.E.C.A.F.	1967 Resolution of F.A.O. Council under Article VI-2 of F.A.O. Constitution	F.A.O., Rome, Italy	F.A.O. Member Nations selected on basis of geographic location, fishing or research activities or other interest in fisheries of Eastern Central Atlantic	Eastern Central Atlantic between Cape Spartel and the Congo River	All	To promote rational utilization of resources; to encourage scientific research and training; to collect and disseminate information
G.F.C.M.	1949 International Agreement under aegis of F.A.O. (Article XIV of F.A.O. Constitution)	F.A.O., Rome, Italy	F.A.O. Member Nations and other Members of United Nations (if approved by two-thirds majority of G.F.C.M.)	Mediterranean Sea and contiguous waters	All	To formulate various aspects of the problems of development and proper utilization of resources; to encourage research and development; to assemble and disseminate information

I.A.T.T.C.	1949 International Convention	La Jolla, California, United States	Signatory States and others by unanimous agreement of Contracting Parties	Eastern Pacific Ocean	Yellowfin and skipjack tuna, fish used as bait for tuna, and other fish taken by tuna vessels	To carry out research on tuna by own research staff; to recommend joint action for conservation
I.C.C.A.T.	1966 International Convention	Madrid, Spain	Members of United Nations or of any specialized agency of the United Nations	Atlantic Ocean, including the adjacent Seas	Tuna and tuna-like fishes and other species exploited in tuna fishing	To carry out studies; to recommend conservation action
I.C.N.A.F.	1949 International Convention, as amended	Dartmouth, Nova Scotia, Canada	Signatory States and others by giving notification of adherence	North-west Atlantic, (eastern limit approximately 42°W Long., southern limit approximately 39°N Lat.). Excluding territorial sea	All, but with particular reference to cod group, flatfish and rosefish	To carry out studies and research; to propose action for stock conservation through closed areas and seasons, size limitation, gear control, catch limits
I.C.S.E.A.F.	1969 International Convention	Not yet fixed	States represented at Conference which adopted the Convention, Members of the United Nations or of any specialized agency of the United Nations, other States unanimously invited by I.C.S.E.A.F.	South-east Atlantic, south of the Congo River, (southern limit parallel 50°S, eastern limit meridian 40°E)	All fish and other living resources, subject to arrangements with other bodies	To carry out studies and research; to make recommendations for joint action, through closed areas and seasons, size limitations, gear control, total catch limits, and other measures

Table 8b.—continued.

BODY	DATE ESTABLISHED AND AUSPICES	HEADQUARTERS	ELIGIBILITY FOR MEMBERSHIP	AREA OF COMPETENCE	RESOURCES COVERED	FUNCTIONS
I.N.P.F.C.	1952 International Convention	Vancouver, B.C., Canada	Signatory States	All waters of North Pacific and adjacent seas. Excluding territorial waters	All, with particular reference to halibut, herring, and salmon	To study fish stocks; to recommend joint conservation action; to administer abstention system
I.O.F.C.	1967 Resolution of the F.A.O. Council under Article VI-1 of the F.A.O. Constitution	F.A.O., Rome, Italy	F.A.O. Member Nations	Indian Ocean and adjacent seas, but excluding the Antarctic area	All	To promote programmes of fishery development and conservation; to encourage research and development activities; to examine management problems
I.P.F.C.	1948 International Agreement under aegis of F.A.O. (Article XIV of F.A.O. Constitution)	F.A.O. Regional Office, Bangkok, Thailand	F.A.O. Member Nations and other Members of the United Nations (if approved by two-thirds majority of I.P.F.C.)	Indo-Pacific area	All	To formulate various aspects of the problems of development and proper utilization of resources; to encourage research and development; to assemble and disseminate information
I.P.H.C.	1953 International Convention	Seattle, Washington, United States	Signatory States	Territorial sea and high seas off western coast of Canada and United States	Halibut (Hippoglossus)	To study halibut stocks; to adopt conservation measures such as catch regulation, size control, open or closed seasons, vessel and gear control, licensing

	Instrument	Headquarters / Meeting	Membership	Area / Waters	Species	Functions
I.P.S.F.C.	1930 International Convention, as amended	New Westminster, B.C., Canada	Signatory States	Fraser river and its tributaries, territorial sea, and high seas off the estuary	Sockeye and pink salmon	To carry out investigations; to adopt conservation measures such as gear control, catch regulation, apportionment of catches
I.W.C.	1946 International Convention, as amended	London, United Kingdom	Signatory States and States giving notification of adherence	All waters in which whaling is prosecuted by factory ships, land stations, and whale catchers	Whale stocks	To promote or carry out studies and research; to adopt conservation measures such as open and closed seasons or areas, size limitation, catch limits
J.K.F.C.	1965 International Agreement	Meets in member countries in rotation	Signatory States	Joint resources survey and regulation zones off the coast of Korea	All	To recommend scientific investigations and conservation measures, including provisional regulatory measures
J.S.F.C.	1956 International Treaty	Meets in member countries in rotation	Signatory States	North-west Pacific, including Sea of Japan, Sea of Okhotsk, and Bering Sea, and excluding territorial waters	All, with particular reference to salmon, trout, and herring	To coordinate joint scientific research programmes; to adopt joint conservation measures, including amount of total catch
M.C.B.S.F.	1959 International Convention	Meets in member countries in rotation	Black Sea States	Black Sea	All	To coordinate scientific research; to develop industrial fishing techniques; to formulate conservation measures

Table 8b.—continued.

Body	Date established and Auspices	Headquarters	Eligibility for Membership	Area of Competence	Resources covered	Functions
N.E.A.F.C.	1959 International Convention	London, United Kingdom	Signatory States and others giving notification of adherence	North-east Atlantic and Arctic Oceans and their dependent seas (western limit approximately 42°W long., southern limit 36°N lat., eastern limit 51°E long.)	All	To keep all fisheries under review; to recommend conservation measures in respect of mesh sizes, size limitation, gear control, closed seasons and areas, amount of total catch or fishing effort
N.P.F.S.C.	1957 International Interim Convention, as amended	Washington, D.C., United States	Signatory States	North Pacific Ocean	Fur seals	To formulate and coordinate research programmes; to recommend conservation measures in respect of size, sex, and age composition of the seasonal commercial kill from a herd, to make recommendations regarding methods of sealing
P.C.S.P.	1952 International Agreement, as supplemented	Secretariat located for four years in each member country in rotation	Signatory States	South Pacific	All	To promote research; to adopt conservation measures including protection of species, open and closed seasons and areas, gear control

S.C.N.E.A.	1957 International Agreement	Meets in member countries in rotation	Signatory States and others acceding to the Agreement with the consent of the Contracting Parties	North-eastern Atlantic, east of Cape Farewell, including the Greenland and Norwegian Seas, the Denmark Strait, the area of Jan Mayen Island and the Barents Sea	Stocks of seals, including the Greenland seal, the hooded seal, and the walrus	To formulate proposals in respect of scientific research and conservation measures, including closed seasons and areas, and total catch quotas
S.C.S.K.	1952 International Agreement	Meets in member countries in rotation	Signatory States	Skagerak and Kattegat waters (bounded on the west by a line from Lindesnes light to Hanstholm light and on the east by the 13th meridian east of Greenwich)	Deep-sea prawns, European lobsters, Norway lobsters and crabs	To coordinate scientific and practical research; to recommend conservation measures

up the Commission is the so-called Schedule, setting out such management measures as size limits, catch limitations, etc. Any changes in these measures—introduction of new regulations, reductions in the catch quota, etc.—are effected by making suitable amendments to this schedule.

Procedurally this is done by some member country making the necessary proposal at the annual meeting of the Commission, after ensuring that the subject has been placed on the agenda sufficiently in advance of the meeting. If the proposal is carried by a two-thirds majority then each of the member countries are, in general, bound to make the necessary national legislative or other arrangements to give legal force to the proposals so far as their nationals are concerned. The exception is that if any country feels strongly that any proposal is unacceptable to it, it can make, within a set period of the recommendation being made, a formal objection to the recommendation. The recommendation then is not binding on that country.

So long as membership of the regional body, and hence compliance with its recommendations, is voluntary, a loophole like this objection procedure is inevitable. Countries will always be afraid that their interests will be ignored by others, and that some unacceptable proposal may be voted into force by the majority. Without the escape route within the formal structure of the Commission, countries could still, if feeling strongly enough, avoid putting the recommendations into effect by withdrawing from the Commission.

Though this arrangement is better than the break-up of the Commission, in fact when the objection procedure is used by one country this is usually followed by objections by other countries, who would otherwise be at a disadvantage. The recommendation then becomes essentially inoperative. Because a very strong recommendation, e.g., for a drastic limit on the current catches, will probably not ever become effective, even if passed by a majority, the recommendations passed tend to be the lowest common denominator among possible management actions. Nevertheless there have been a good number of occasions, especially when the scientific or other evidence has given clear guidance as to the action to be taken, and this action is simple and non-discriminating, when these arrangements of Commissions have resulted in good management actions, e.g., most regulations in the North Atlantic; control of the Pacific halibut and salmon fisheries.

The Commissions listed in *Table 8b* have thus been effective in deciding on and recommending a range of important measures. Usually these decisions are taken by the Commission as a whole, e.g., all members of the International Whaling Commission discuss and vote on the level of the total catch of Antarctic baleen whales, even though less than half the member countries are actively engaged in Antarctic whaling. Some Commissions have, however, found that their field of responsibility is so large and complex that it has to be subdivided, and the initial proposals for action in a particular area or in regard to a particular stock are taken by the sub-committee or other subsidiary bodies with responsibility for that area or stock. For example, I.C.N.A.F. has divided the whole area defined by its Convention into five sub-areas, each of which is the responsibility of a particular panel. The International Commission for the Conservation of Atlantic Tuna has set up similar panels, but with responsibility divided according (mainly) to the species, i.e., for yellowfin tuna and skipjack; for albacore and bluefin in the North Atlantic; for albacore and bluefin in the South Atlantic, and for other species. In each case panel membership is limited to countries with a direct interest in the relevant area or species. In this way the discussions and decisions are in the first instance limited to those directly concerned, though subject to final approval by the whole Commission.

While this has provided a satisfactory machinery for most management decisions—though in too many cases the machinery has not been used as much or as effectively as it might have been —the open and multi-sided decisions involved in the operation of most Commissions have not been entirely satisfactory when a substantial amount of bargaining and horse-trading is involved. The commission machinery works well in regard to uniform and basically non-discriminatory measures, such as minimum mesh sizes or the level of the total catch that may be taken. It is less satisfactory in regard to possible division or allocation of the total allowable catch.

Commissions can help in providing a forum for general discussions on what principles could be used in such allocation. I.C.N.A.F., indeed, through its Standing Committee on Regulatory Measures, has in fact established some fairly definite guidelines. Under these, some given proportion of the total quota is divided according to historic performance, i.e., the average percentage of the total catch taken by each country over some previous period or periods (there was considered to be some advantage in considering both a fairly long period, e.g. ten years, and a short period such as the immediately preceding two or three years). The rest of the allowable catch might then be allocated on the base of so-called 'special interests', i.e., to coastal states, to states heavily dependent on fisheries, or those developing their fisheries, for whom past performance would be a bad guide to present or potential future interest in a stock. These are, however, only guidelines. Decisions on any actual allocation of a specific overall quota must be a matter of hard bargaining. The chances of this bargaining being successful is increased if it is not carried out in public and if the number of participants is limited. This really means a meeting of those directly concerned, outside the Commission, and this procedure is to a greater or lesser extent formally accepted or even encouraged by most Commissions. For example, the arrangements for division of the Antarctic baleen whale quota was made between the five countries then whaling (Japan, Netherlands, Norway, U.K., and U.S.S.R.) outside the framework of the I.W.C.

The Inter-American Tropical Tuna Commission, which controls the tuna fishery (principally for yellowfin) in the Eastern Pacific, commonly interrupts its sessions after a provisional figure for an allowable catch has been reached, for a separate inter-governmental meeting which discusses how particular national interests can be accommodated within the total. Several other Commissions specifically exclude questions of allocation of national shares from their field of competence. However, although these questions of allocation and division of any overall quota may not be discussed in the Commissions, the success of these discussions, and indeed their existence, are in large part due to the work of the Commissions. These have often provided the occasions at which the necessary discussions can take place and also, and perhaps most important, the formal Commission meetings have enabled the various senior fisheries administrators in different countries to know each other, and get used to working together.

ENFORCEMENT

Even after the biological and economic analyses are completed, and the best course of action has been identified and recommended, no benefits will arise until the action is actually undertaken—a larger mesh size is used in the trawl nets, or the amount of fishing is reduced. Enforcement of the regulations is therefore an essential part of any programme of fishery management.

So far as national fisheries are concerned enforcement of regulations related to fishery management is not different in principle from the enforcement of any other set of rules and regulations. Practical difficulties arise because when a fisherman is at sea fishing in the middle of the North Sea he is not under the eye of the local policeman. Therefore as far as possible the fishermen are persuaded that to follow the regulations would be in their own best interests. Where legal sanctions are imposed these preferably relate to actions or misdeeds that can be checked when the vessel is in port, and for which therefore evidence can be obtained without too much difficulty. For example, in England it is not an offence to catch an undersized fish, but it is an offence to retain it on board, and in particular to expose it for sale, i.e., on the fish market among the rest of the catch. Even so there are a number of important measures that cannot be controlled solely from shore. The use of a small mesh can be discouraged by the prevention of the landing of small fish, and the presence on board of small-meshed nets can be controlled by inspection before sailing and after return. What cannot be controlled on shore is the use of chafers or the placing of liners inside the net. Two cod-ends of legal mesh, one inside the other, will retain almost the same quantity of small fish as a cod-end of half the legal mesh-size. Checking on such malpractices requires direct inspection of the fishing operations at sea. Most countries now have one or more fishery inspection or protection vessels, which include among their duties such inspections of fishing operations at sea.

However good the control, fishermen are quite capable of breaking any rules if they are convinced that it is in their interests to do so, and particularly if they believe that other fishermen are already flouting the rules. The need not only for rules to be kept, but to be seen to be kept, is especially important in international fisheries. Fishermen are naturally very suspicious of the misdeeds, or supposed misdeeds, of foreigners, and are very ready to believe that the French (or the Russians or the English, as the case may be) are sweeping the seas clean of all fish, however small, by the use of meshes well below the internationally agreed minimum size. From this suspicion it is a short step to considering that if the French (or whoever) are breaking the agreements, everyone else has a right to do the same.

Some machinery is therefore needed to ensure that the fishermen of one country have a guarantee that fishermen of other countries are abiding by the international agreements and recommendations. Ideally this might take the form of full international enforcement, with international control vessels operated by the appropriate international body inspecting fishing vessels of the member countries, and imposing penalties for any infractions. In most areas such a solution is still a long way off, but the main objectives, of assuring fishermen that other countries are playing the game according to rules, can be achieved with inspection only, without direct rights of prosecution or of imposing penalties.

Such international inspection is now coming into operation in several parts of the world. Most encouraging is the North Atlantic, because this is an area with some of the most complex fisheries, including countries with very different political systems and political and economic interests. Parallel schemes have been introduced by the two regional bodies, I.C.N.A.F. and N.E.A.F.C., under which an inspection vessel, carrying a duly authorized inspection officer can stop a fishing vessel of any other member country, even on the high seas, inspect its nets and catch, and if any infraction is found—nets with too small meshes, undersized fish, etc.—report this to the Government of the fishing vessel, which will then take appropriate action. At present this scheme is incomplete, since certain countries do not allow foreign inspectors to go below decks. For these countries inspecting, and inspection, is limited to the fish and gear on deck. More complex inspection procedures will be necessary for the further international management measures now being introduced or being actively considered. For example, proposals for catch quotas, especially if allocated to countries, will require a check not only on the methods of fishing, but on the quantity of catch. For this some standard recording system such as a log book would appear to be necessary. However, a good start has been made on international inspection, which together with necessary national enforcement, including appropriate legal measures, should ensure that once management measures have been identified and recommended, they will be in fact carried out.

REFERENCES

BEVERTON, R. J. H., and HODDER, V. M. (1962), 'Report of the working group of scientists on fishery assessment in relation to regulation problems', *Ann. Proc. int. Commn. N.W. Atlant. Fish.*, **11**, suppl.

CHAPMAN, D. G. (1964), 'Reports of the Committee of Three Scientists on the special scientific investigation of the Antarctic whale stocks', *Rep. int. Commn. Whale*, **14**, 32–106.

INTERNATIONAL COMMISSION FOR N.W. ATLANTIC FISHERIES (1968), 'Report of the working group on joint biological and economic assessment of conservation actions', *Ann. Proc. int. Commn. N.W. Atlant. Fish.*, **17**, 48–84.

Chapter

8

MANAGEMENT OF FISHERIES—
THE FUTURE

IT HAS become a commonplace in the specialized literature of the fisheries that the management of world fisheries is approaching a crisis. The cause of this crisis is the growing imbalance between the capacity of the world's fishing fleets, and the resources, at least of the more familiar types of fish, available to them. Since 1945 there has been a continual expansion in the world fish catches, which have doubled approximately every ten years. This has been achieved by a widespread improvement in the techniques of catching, processing, and marketing fish. The most obvious example has been the development of the long-range fishing fleets, either of independent vessels, such as the monster 5000 ton Japanese stern trawlers capable of catching and processing over 100 tons of fish a day, or the self-contained fleets of catching, processing, supply, and transport vessels of the U.S.S.R. Equally important have been the somewhat less spectacular improvements in methods of fish detection and capture that have greatly increased the efficiency of local fleets, and the developments of freezing and other methods of processing which have given these fleets access to world-wide markets. Freed from the vagaries of a limited local market, and having the prospect of a good price however much fish they catch, many local fisheries have had every incentive to increase their size and capacity.

Whereas the fisheries have expanded significantly, the fishery resources are limited, although so far, taking the world as a whole, the demand for fish, and the capacity for catching it, have been less than the potential of the resource. A recent study (Gulland, 1972), has estimated the potential annual catches of the more familiar types of fish as some 100 million tons (*see Table* 9).

Table 9.—POTENTIAL ANNUAL YIELDS (million tons) FROM MAJOR GROUPS OF FISH, AND RECENT CATCHES. (*From* Gulland, 1972.)

	TEMPERATE AREAS				TROPICAL AREAS			TOTAL
	North Atlantic	North Pacific	South Atlantic	South Pacific	Atlantic	Pacific	Indian Ocean	
Large pelagic*	Trace	0·6	‖	‖	1·1	1·9	0·7	4·3
Demersal†	10·6	3·5	4·9	0·8	2·9	12·4	7·4	42·5
Shoaling pelagic‡	10·3	5·7	6·7	12·3	4·9	7·7	6·0	53·6
Crustaceans§	0·3	0·4	0·1	0·1	0·4	0·8	0·2	2·3
TOTAL	21·2	10·2	11·7	13·2	8·9	22·8	14·3	102·7
(1970 catches)	15·4	8·0	4·1	9·5	3·3	12·7	2·7	55·7

* Tunas and salmon;
† E.g., cod, plaice, rockfishes, sea-breams, and rays;
‡ E.g., herring, anchovy, and mackerels;
§ Shrimps, crabs, and lobsters;
‖ Included in corresponding tropical areas.

The total living resources of the seas that might ultimately be harvested by man are much larger than the resources listed in the table, and include for example the krill in the Antarctic, from which tens, or possibly hundreds, of millions of tons could be taken annually once the technology has been developed for catching and processing it at an economically acceptable price. However, fishing as it is known at present, and which has produced the steady increases in world catch, depends, and will depend in the foreseeable future, on the types of fish listed in the table. Clearly, the past rate of increase cannot continue for much longer. A direct extrapolation at some 7 per cent per year implies that by the middle of the next decade world catches would exceed the available potential.

In the past similar situations have arisen in respect of particular stocks of fish, e.g., the bottom fish in the North Sea at the beginning of this century, where continuing developments in the fisheries have met the limit set by the productivity of the resource. Though there have been failures to achieve proper management of such fisheries, the impact of such failures has been reduced by the diversion of the surplus effort to other stocks, e.g. the expansion of the British distant water fishing to Iceland and Bear Island. Such diversion will not be possible when most of the world's fish stocks have become fully exploited, and this will happen soon. Nevertheless the pressures which have resulted in the post-war developments—a growing human population; the need of most of these people for increased supply of protein per head; and greater technological ability to catch, process, and market fish—will continue undiminished. There will therefore be no alternative to positive management of these stocks, and the future health of world fisheries will depend on how the various processes (of scientific research, and choice of implementation of regulatory measures) discussed in this book can be carried out.

Of the different groups, the scientists are probably in the best shape to face the approaching challenge. The techniques outlined in Chapter 4 have proved adequate to give useful advice in a wide range of fisheries, though this does not mean that they could not be improved. To an excessive degree the methods consider the individual species in isolation, without considering the entire eco-system in which they live. This makes them less efficient in dealing with multi-species fisheries, or with separate fisheries exploiting different stocks in the same area which possibly interact, e.g., one species feeding on another, and is likely also to make less realistic and reliable the studies of single species fisheries.

These traditional methods also rely to a large extent on measuring the effects of established fisheries, while management measures will be most effective and least painful if they can be introduced early. This requires some scientific advice before the fishery is well developed, but good scientific techniques for providing this are still lacking. This tendency for management measures to be introduced too late because of the timing of the scientific studies has been strengthened in the past both by the professional attitudes of the scientists, who like to be sure of their ground before offering advice, and by the willingness of too many administrators to use these attitudes as an excuse for postponing action. There is now a growing awareness of the need for changes in these matters (Gulland, 1971).

A cause for more serious shortcomings in scientific advice, both now and probably in the future, is the shortage of scientists of the right type—familiar with the biological complexities of the life of fish in the sea, and having the mathematical dexterity to carry out the necessary quantitative analyses—and of the data for them to use. Though fish population dynamics is a comparatively old subject, dating from Baranov's work in Russia in 1918, the number of practitioners is still very small, and they are mainly limited to a few major centres—particularly the borders of the North Sea, western North America, and Japan. This shortage places a heavy burden on those few scientists with proven capacity in fish population dynamics. The large number of international fishery meetings held each year, including small working groups to assess the states of various stocks and the sessions of the relevant regional fishery bodies, are largely attended by the same few people. This leaves little time for basic scientific studies in their home laboratories by those concerned, but familiarity with each other does help toward discussions. Provided the scientific studies do get done, the shortage of experienced scientists may not, in itself, be a severe drawback from the point of view of world fisheries.

However, the fact that many countries do not have relevant scientific expertise of their own can be serious. They therefore have to accept the advice of foreign experts over matters that may critically affect their fisheries. However competent these scientists may be, and however matters are arranged to eliminate any suggestion of bias or prejudice in their advice, a country's confidence in this advice is bound to be less than when its own national scientists can participate in the preparation and interpretation of the advice. Any lack of confidence must hinder the introduction of timely and adequate management measures.

Numerous scientists of the highest standard representing all the countries involved are still not sufficient to ensure good scientific advice. They must have data to work with. The basic data required for most analyses are quite limited. Knowledge of the total catch removed from each stock is essential, and little can be done without some estimate of the effort or catch-per-unit effort, and of the sizes or ages of fish being caught. A range of other studies are likely to be useful in sharpening preliminary analyses, based only on catch and effort data, but such information, e.g., on changes in the physical or chemical environment, is unlikely to be of much help unless the basic catch, effort, and size composition data are already available.

Although the basic data is fairly easy and cheap to collect—a few technicians visiting the fish markets each morning to interview the fishermen as they land, and to measure samples of fish is all that is strictly necessary, and they cost much less than even a moderate sized research vessel—it is not being collected on anything like a sufficient scale. Nor is the attention being paid to the dull matters of collecting catch statistics, or measuring fish, increasing at such a rate as to give much confidence that the situation will greatly improve in the near future. Sixty years ago, when the International Council for the Exploration of the Sea was founded, priority was given to building up a good statistical system, and from its early years I.C.E.S. has published an annual *Bulletin Statistique*, giving the catches of each species in each country in each area of the I.C.E.S. region. Very soon this became close to being achieved, but since then progress has been comparatively slight. Certain gaps and inconsistencies in the catch data, e.g., concerning the areas in which some of the Spanish catches are taken, still remain, while information on the size of fish being caught remains extremely patchy. Outside the I.C.E.S. region, statistics in the I.C.N.A.F. area have reached about the same standard—again with very large gaps in the provision of size-composition data—but elsewhere statistical data are extremely incomplete. F.A.O. is providing an increasing amount of regional data, in addition to the summary world data contained in the *Yearbooks of Fishery Statistics*, particularly in relation to its various regional bodies. These data are published at intervals in various *Bulletins of Fishery Statistics*, but with some exceptions the basic statistics at the national level are not so good as in the North Atlantic.

A fundamental change in the attitude towards the collection of the basic data seems necessary. Instead of an afterthought, provided as and when opportunity occurs, or when the need for such data has been clearly established, the collection of basic statistical and biological data, and the provision of it to the appropriate regional or other international body needs to be considered as a major responsibility of anyone exploiting a fishery resource. If, and only if, this is done, will scientists be able to provide adequate advice to those concerned with fishery management.

The other problem related to the scientific advice is one of attitude, and is related to the question of timeliness discussed below. Scientists like to have their studies complete before exposing them to the possibly critical outside world and therefore hesitate to give advice until the studies are finished. Administrators are often glad to use the absence of definite scientific advice as an excuse for inaction. What both often forget is that in the early stages of a fishery, advice need not be precise, and the data then available, albeit rather rough, may be perfectly adequate for guidance on management measures. Scientists therefore need to be more forthcoming in making statements, even hedged about with qualification, as early as possible in the history of a fishery, even if the data is not conclusive enough to provide the firm results required for publication in the normal scientific literature.

OBJECTIVES

The same problem of attitude or of education, rather than of absence of data or of basic theoretical techniques, arises in relation to the objectives of management. Since so much of the study of the problems of fisheries management has been done by biologists a feeling has developed that it is chiefly or wholly a biological problem, and that the main, or even the only, objective of management should be the protection or conservation of the fish stock or the harvesting of the maximum sustained yield measured in physical terms. Obviously if the resource is destroyed, that will be the end of the fishery, but the continued existence of the fish stocks is no guarantee of a healthy fishery. Failure to take a sufficiently broad view of the objectives of management can result in over-restrictive regulations that prevent the development of an efficient fishery, e.g., the banning of the most effective type of gear. Paradoxically it may also result in a delay in the introduction of management measures. So long as preservation of the stock is the only objective, action can wait until the stocks become clearly threatened. Particularly in a rapidly developing fishery this may not happen until the fishing fleet and shore installations have grown far beyond the desirable level for the productive capacity of the resource. With or without management action there must then be a painful period of re-adjustment as the fleet contracts to its optimum size.

The need for this re-adjustment can be minimized if action is taken during the development period to avoid over-expansion. In this respect management and development should be considered as two interacting aspects of the same process, of making the best use of the fishery resources. This view of management is gaining ground, as is the view that the objectives should be quite broadly defined. The rather academic discussions on the relative virtues of the maximum sustained physical yield or the maximum net economic yield as the proper objective can then be avoided. Attention can then be concentrated on the practical problems of managing the fisheries to ensure that the best social and economic use is made of the very considerable living resources of the sea.

The techniques currently available to manage the fisheries (catch quotas, size limits, etc.) probably provide the manager with a sufficient array of tools to tackle most of the problems currently arising. It is likely that more use will be made of the direct methods of controlling the input into the fisheries, e.g., by licensing a limited number of vessels, or allocating catch quotas, rather than indirect methods, which reduce the efficiency of the operations, e.g., the banning of highly efficient gear, or the introduction of closed seasons. Less emphasis is likely to be given to such matters as control of mesh sizes or limits of the sizes of fish that can be landed. These changes are matters of differences in balance and do not introduce any fundamentally new problems. One problem that may become more prominent arises in connexion with the use of catch quotas to control the amount of fishing. For practical and administrative reasons, catch quotas, allocated or not, are becoming the most common method of control. This requires that the quota needs to be revised regularly—probably at least annually—to take into account changes in the abundance of the fish stocks, particularly for non-fishery reasons, such as year-class changes. These adjustments to the quotas should be as responsive as possible to changes in abundance, so that, for example, the quota is increased as soon as a good year-class enters the fishery.

The major problems in the fields of fishery management are rather those of the mechanics of implementing appropriate measures. Two in particular can be identified, though not so readily solved. The first arises in a developing fishery, and is the assurance of the timely introduction of management measures. The other applies more particularly to an established fishery, in which proper management could reduce the costs of fishing well below the value of the catch; the question then is who should get these spoils. If an explicit decision on this is not made and action taken accordingly, it is most probable that whatever the short-term effect, in the long run the spoils will disappear in excessive costs—compare, for example, the ever-shortening open season when the control is by a single unallocated quota.

Both these involve questions of jurisdiction and authority. Without a strong controlling authority it is unlikely that management action will be taken until it is quite clear that it is necessary, which is usually too late for it to be painless. The simplest method of distributing the profit from a well-managed resource is for it to go in the first instance to the body exercising jurisdiction over the fishery.

Lately there have been extensive discussions on the question of jurisdiction over fisheries, and over the seas in general, and these will grow to a climax during the United Nations Conference on the Law of the Sea, scheduled for 1974. This Conference will, among other things, attempt to resolve the many disputes and uncertainties about jurisdiction. In particular some decision may be reached between the various views as to what the pattern of jurisdiction may be, including some new form of international authority over high seas fisheries, or a strengthening of the present pattern of regional fishery bodies and commissions.

To a large extent these discussions are irrelevant to the question of how successfully the world's fisheries will be managed in the future. In whatever way the arguments are resolved, it is quite clear that there will be a much greater authority over fisheries, whether national or international, than in the past. The question then is, How well will this authority be used? The decisions on the pattern of jurisdiction will have a vital effect on particular fishing enterprises; for example, a wide extension of national jurisdiction would have a crippling effect on long-range fisheries such as those of U.S.S.R. or Japan, unless the countries or companies concerned can reach agreements with the coastal states. In the short run a wide extension of national jurisdiction combined with exclusive fishing rights could lead to a drop in world fish catch until the coastal states concerned develop the catching and handling capacity to replace the existing long-range fleets. In the long run the same questions of how to maintain the rate of fishing at its optimum level will have to be solved by whatever authority exists. There has been in the past no evidence that national authorities perform any better, or any worse, then international authorities, provided the latter do have sufficient power, and there seems no reason to suppose that there would be any significant differences in the future. What is to be hoped is that in the future the growing understanding of the various problems—scientific, economic, social, and political—of fisheries management will result in the authorities concerned being able to ensure a better use of the fish resources of the world. In this understanding it is hoped that this volume will play some small part.

REFERENCES

GULLAND, J. A. (1971), 'Science and fishery management', *J. Cons. int. Explor. Mer*, **33**(3), 471–477.

GULLAND, J. A. (1972), *The Fish Resources of the Oceans*. London: Fishing News (Books) Ltd.

AUTHOR INDEX

SUBJECT INDEX

193